THE SKILLS OF NEGOTIATING

Bill Scott

WILDWOOD HOUSE

First published 1981 by Gower Publishing Company Limited
Aldershot, Hampshire
Reprinted 1982, 1983, 1984

Reprinted 1986 by
Wildwood House Limited
Gower House
Croft Road
Aldershot
Hampshire GU11 3HR
England

British Library Cataloguing in Publication Data

Scott, Bill 1925–
   The skills of negotiating—(Management skills library)
   1. Negotiation in business
   I. Title   II. Series
   658.4′5   HD58.6

ISBN 0-7045-0554-1

Printed and bound in Great Britain by
Biddles Ltd, Guildford and King's Lynn

Contents

Preface

This book is about negotiating.

More specifically the book is about the *skills* used in negotiating, with the word 'skill' used to describe personal abilities, as distinct from the rules, regulations and laws governing negotiations.

The skills include a range of behaviours which can become instinctive for the experienced negotiator; but often, his behaviour has developed over a long period during which he may never have had the opportunity or the ability to sit back and evaluate his competence. He has not been able to check whether he be satisfied with his skills, to see whether they need a little polishing, or to see gaps where he might be able to develop his repertoire. The book is intended for him, as much as for the less experienced person, freshly venturing into the field of negotiations.

The shape of the book

The book is in three main parts.

In the first part, the emphasis is on a pattern of negotiation which will produce the greatest possible agreement to the advantage of both parties. The skills in this part are those which help the parties to work together, creatively, *Towards Agreement.*

A different pattern of negotiation is sometimes needed, calling for different skills. Because of a particular strategic situation, or because of the approach of the other party, the focus may be on building a distinct advantage for one's own party. Part II of the book accordingly looks at the measures and countermeasures when the parties have this concern for their independent benefit. The theme here is negotiating *To Our Advantage* — words carefully chosen to distinguish from the more belligerent line of 'winning battles', to which we devote a separate chapter.

In the first two parts of the book, then, we shall be concerned with 'how to build the largest cake' and with 'how to earn the tastier share.'

Part III deals with other ingredients in the *Mastery* of negotiating abilities. Those ingredients include some skills which are needed whatever pattern we negotiate in; they include the taking of strategic decisions which will be influenced by the style of the other party to the negotiation, the country and culture from which they come, and the strategic setting of the negotiations; and they include the influence of the negotiator's boss.

The origins of the book

This book provides a framework which has been developed and tested with some 400 negotiators from many different types of business, in many different countries. The book owes much to their wisdom and experience.

The foundations were laid when I was asked by a Scandinavian client to help the rapid development of their international business. Their executives had increasingly to conduct their business in a second language, and in many different countries. I was at first surprised to find how helpful they found some of the ideas which are here described; and subsequently, when I used the ideas with international bankers, with insurance brokers, with the oil industry, with the electrical industry, with the engineering industry and with retail chains, I was pleased to find confirmation and further development of the thinking.

In the course of developing the ideas, I sought for helpful literature. The literature I found was of two kinds: theoretical treatments of negotiations, principally as mathematical or psychological exercises; and books which were apparently practical but which treated negotiation as a grand combat, often highlighting methods and tricks which my clients did not find appropriate for their business dealings. I was unable to find a book which both treated negotiation in a practical way and reflected the constructive and creative skills of the negotiators with whom I work.

This book is designed to fill that gap. It is intended to provide a simple statement of the practical skills of successful negotiators.

W. P. Scott
February, 1981

12 Trafalgar Road,
Southport,
England

Acknowledgements

Knut Aabol

Stella Ascott

Sven Söderberg

Malcolm Stern

David Sutton

Bryan Tattersall

Penny Aitken

Part I

Towards agreement

Prologue

A negotiation is a form of meeting between two parties: Our Party and the Other Party.

The objective of most negotiations is to reach an agreement, and the aim in this first part of the book is to cover the skills of creative negotiations, in which both parties together move towards an outcome which is good, in their joint interest.

The foundations for such creative negotiation are very soon laid. They depend on first establishing a co-operative climate (chapter 1) and then going on to start the negotiation in a way which leads the two parties to work together harmoniously and creatively (chapter 2).

The negotiation proper then gets under way. It is often a dramatic and exciting period with the shape and form of the meeting being sometimes difficult to predict or to control. But there is a constant fabric to negotiations, and in chapter 3 we identify some of the main threads in the fabric.

It is those threads which we need to make use of, if we are to control the negotiation 'Towards Agreement' (chapter 4), and there are a range of tactics which can help (chapter 5).

Effective communication is an essential element of effective negotiation; the skills of effective communication are an essential part of the equipment of skilled negotiators (chapter 6).

The progress of the negotiation 'Towards Agreement' depends on the foundations being carefully laid. But before they can be carefully laid the ground must have been skilfully prepared (chapter 7).

In this first part of the book the experienced negotiator will find much which is within his common practice and much which confirms the wisdom of what he already does, as well as impulses to new or improved behaviour. For the less experienced negotiator it offers a firm foundation on which to build his abilities.

1 Creating the climate

There is some climate or atmosphere which pervades any negotiation.

The climate of one negotiation may be tough, uncompromising, tense. Of another negotiation, low key, long winded, time consuming. Of a third, warm, creative, friendly. Of a fourth, cold, formal and precise.

All negotiators recognise these differences of climate or atmosphere but are sometimes puzzled as to how they arise.

In this chapter we shall be concerned with the questions:

When and how is the climate created?
What can we do about it?
What can we learn from the way the Other Party starts behaving?

At later stages in the book, we will be concerned with more fundamental, psychological and strategic reasons governing the type of climate which the negotiators should seek to create. But within this chapter we are concerned with the issues of "how to", not yet with issues of "why".

The critical period

The critical period in forming the climate is short — very short. Possibly a matter of seconds, certainly not more than minutes.

Within this very short period, from the parties coming together at the outset of negotiations, an atmosphere has been created which is very durable, and almost impossible to improve subsequently. The mood has become warm or cold, co-operative or suspicious, collaborative or defensive. The pace has become brisk or lethargic. The pattern of precedence — who talks, how much — has been asserted. The tactics of the respective Parties have probably been made visible, and may even have been recognised by the Other Party.

Of course, these aspects of the climate are not only influenced by what happens in the first few moments — they are also influenced by what has happened in the preliminaries, before Parties meet and possibly also by what happens subsequently during the negotiation. But the impressions generated in the opening moments are much stronger than those generated beforehand, and can quickly erase them.

Some development of the climate will take place during the meeting, but that climate which was established at the outset remains of critical importance. It forms the level around which there will be some modulations, but not any major positive development. (Exceptionally, if there are traumatic developments which the Parties manage to overcome, a new and positive climate may be possible — but at this stage we are not looking forward to traumas!)

There can be deterioration from the climate initially established and to prevent that, we need to take positive steps during the negotiation.

But the key to the climate of a negotiation lies in what happens within the opening moments. It is therefore important for us to look closely into what happens in those opening moments and into what we can do in them to create a good climate.

The process of creating the climate

Let us first consider what obviously happens when two Parties first come together to negotiate.

They meet and greet one another. They open some pattern of conversation and within a minute or two find themselves seated at the bargaining table, beginning to talk business.

Already the negotiator, apart from what he sees, is beginning to feel some reaction about the negotiation. Maybe, 'It is going to be one of those awful bores'; or maybe, 'Boy, I'll have to keep on my toes with these people'; or even, 'This feels as though it could be really productive'.

The more obvious elements of the meeting/greeting/ seating ritual do not adequately explain why this mood should have come about, and we need to look deeper.

In fact, the brain has received a much greater range of impulses than those which have been consciously recognised. It has noted visually the way in which the Other Party has come in, the non-verbal elements of eye-contact and of posture and of gesture. It has been influenced by the pace and pattern of movement, and by the pace and tone of voice used in discussion. It has been influenced too by the topics which have been explored during this early discussion.

These are impulses picked up by the sub-conscious and then interpreted. The pattern of interpretation depends on the situation which existed immediately beforehand: typically a situation in which at least one party would feel uncertain and insecure, suspicious and even defensive.

Moreover, each party comes from a different immediate experience and often from a difficult immediate experience — the one, of the particular hell he has been experiencing in his office, and the other from the different sort of hell in travelling to that office.

There is thus a wealth of impulses, not immediately obvious and likely to be interpreted unconsciously in ways which may well be negative.

There is every prospect, unless skilled steps are taken, that the negotiation will get off to a bad start.

Influencing the climate

Before considering the means by which we want to influence the climate we must first consider what sort of climate we want to create.

At this stage of the book, our theme is to create a process of negotiating Towards Agreement. To that end, the main characteristics of the climate we want to create need to be:

- cordial
- collaborative
- brisk
- businesslike.

It takes time to achieve a collaborative mood. It is no use immediately confronting the business aspects of the meeting. The two parties need sufficient time to get on the same wavelength – to adjust their thinking and their behaviour to one another.

For this reason, it is desirable that the topics at the outset should be neutral, non-business. For example, they might be:

- immediate experiences – the sort of journey that the visitor has had; the ground he has covered, the people he has met, and so on.
- topics from the outside – the football, the ice hockey, the golf, or even (as long as it is not too dismal) this morning's newspaper headline.
- personal interests, showing real concern to find out his interests, without threatening. For example, to the opening question 'How are you?' , give and get on the personal level. Reply along the lines 'I'm feeling very relaxed. I've been spending the weekend fishing, which I greatly enjoy. What have you been doing?'
- for negotiators who have dealt with one another previously, some shared social experience or joint success.

This opening discussion enables the parties to adjust verbally to one another and to begin a meeting of minds.

Whilst it is going on, the non-verbal messages are passing

equally as strongly. The first impression is that of a figure. The figure has a posture which may convey confidence or uncertainty, liveliness or lethargy, relaxation or tension. The key elements of posture conveying these impressions are respectively the head, the back and the shoulders. In addition to the figure's posture, it is seen to be clothed in some way: bright or dark; conformist or non-conformist; neat or scruffy. (For further reading on these matters, see reference 1 in the reading list at the end of this book.)

Putting these thoughts into practice, I am guided by three thoughts:

1 As a businessman, I am expected to be reasonably neat and well groomed.
2 As an English businessman, I am expected to wear a dark suit.
3 As a visitor to countries with formal customs (such as Norway or France), most businessmen expect me to be formal. So I try to be well groomed, and always wear a dark suit. But when visiting less formal countries (such as Sweden or Denmark), dress is less important. It is still important for me to be well groomed; but slacks and blazer are as acceptable as a dark suit.

The instant impression of a figure is very soon reinforced by other impressions; most powerfully, by eye-contact. There is great power in the form of the first eye-contact between the parties. Each sees the form of this eye-contact as open or furtive; trustworthy or suspect.

Other influences are the expressions, and the sort of gestures which are being used. There are elements too of touch — the handclasp may be interpreted as forceful or slimy or reasonable. In Western society, the gesture of putting one's left hand on Other Party's shoulder while shaking hands with the right hand, is interpreted either as exuberant 'He's over-acting — I had better watch it') or as powerseeking ('That's a strong thrust — he is trying to dominate me').

Even smell may come into it — there is one otherwise brilliant negotiator whom I just cannot tolerate because nobody seems to have suggested that he should occasionally take a bath.

The pace of a meeting is also established right at the outset. It is evidenced first by the pace at which people move towards the initial greeting — the speed with which the visitor enters the room, the speed at which the host rises from his desk or moves forward. Then by the pace at which the parties talk with one another. In this establishment of the pace, the most common difficulty is uncertainty about what to say, so that pauses and gaps occur, which pave the way towards a slow momentum throughout the negotiating process. But the opposite, flustered and hurried, creates an equally bad starting point. 'Brisk and businesslike' is what we seek.

These preliminaries — the discussion and the non-verbal impressions — set the tone and mood. There is a strong case for carrying out these preliminaries whilst standing up, before moving to the negotiating table. This is in part because the social skills can often be practised more easily whilst standing than whilst seated. For example, whilst standing, it is on the one hand easier to change the angle of contact and to move nearer or further away, compared to the seated position where the distance cannot easily be changed, and where often the seating arrangements are those of eyeball to eyeball confrontation. Moreover the move from standing to sitting can be used to emphasise the move from the climate formation element of the meeting into the businesslike environment of the meeting, and so give force to the development of the businesslike character. Provided always that the opening climate formation has been completed whilst still standing.

The duration of this opening period — the ice-breaking period, as it is often called — deserves a little thought. There is a tension between the concern of both parties to get as quickly as possible into business, and the unspoken need to take sufficient time to adjust to one another. As a yardstick for consideration, I suggest thinking of 5 per cent of the time for any negotiation being given up to the ice-breaking. That is, if we are going to have a meeting lasting one hour, think in terms of three minutes. If we are going to have a meeting lasting over several days, then go out to dinner together on the evening before the first business meeting.

The climate formation period is particularly important when there are teams (not just individuals) coming to the negotiating forum. When two teams of four meet for the first time there is first a crowd scene of introductions and handshaking. There is likely to be a confused period with very little genuine communication between the parties. If, after the seconds it takes to complete the round of hand-shaking, the parties then assemble in a circle of eight people, there will immediately be a cold atmosphere with one or two individuals making lonely noises, the rest embarrassed and uninvolved.

More positive atmospheres develop when people come together in smaller groups. The eight can readily split into two or three groups, each with two or three people mixed from the different teams. Within these smaller groupings, there can be — indeed there is likely to be — an immediate hum of conversation. This friendly hum is heard as a background by all eight, and is felt to create a warm process of communication from the outset.

Learning from opening moves

The opening moves in one sense set the climate for the relationship between the parties. In another sense, they offer us information about the character, attitudes and intentions of Other Party.

At this stage, these impressions about Other Party must still be interpreted cautiously. Nevertheless we shall soon have to take important procedural steps which will have lasting sway in the conduct of the negotiations and on our respective form of influence within them. We shall, hopefully, have prepared our ground thoughtfully but flexibly (using methods to be discussed fully in chapter 7), and we must now try to make use of the information which is available from his opening behaviour, before we sit down to business.

We can quickly pick up such clues to two different aspects of the negotiator : clues to his experience and skill, and clues to his style.

His *experience and skill* will be shown by the non-verbal clues. By his posture, his expression, and by the extent to which he makes positive use of the ice-breaking period. If he is hesitant about the opening greetings, or if he is bursting to break into the business of the meeting – then we are dealing with someone who is not expert in negotiating. Attention to the human element is a trait of the skilled negotiator.

His *style* will be shown by the form of discussions during the opening period. In particular, an experienced negotiator who is searching for co-operation between the parties will focus on neutral topics. A different experienced negotiator, seeking to enhance his power, will behave quite differently: he will from the outset be probing to identify the strengths of our business situation, the weaknesses of that situation, to find out where our priorities and concerns lie. Not only Our situation but also, at the personal level, My situation. What I value, what I am confident about, what I am concerned about, how he can exploit Me.

Information on those topics is important to the negotiator seeking to manoeuvre in his own interests, at the expense of our interests. He perceives the information as giving him an edge in subsequent negotiations. And indeed he is right, if the game is to be played by the unspoken rules for gaining advantage to one side.

If we see these symobls of possible combat then we have to be careful. We cannot yet be sure of how the negotiation will unfold but we can now see an amber light. It is not yet that red light which could tell us that Other Party was going to force a battle; it may just be that he is nervous, or inexperienced or tired.

It may be of course that he is warlike – that the amber is switching to red – and it is all too easy for us to respond defensively, take on our own warrior's garb and enter into battle.

But at this stage we are not sure what his behaviour means. We are starting with the intention of creating an agreement oriented climate if we can. Our behaviour needs to press towards the cordial and the collaborative; to give him further chance to adapt to that mood; and to give ourselves more time and ability to judge how he wants to respond.

Our technique now should aim to deflect the fighting thrusts and to concentrate on the cordial. We must keep trying to concentrate on neutral topics and possibly to move more towards his welfare.

Consider this opening dialogue:

'Welcome. How nice to see you.'
'Great to be here. Tell me, how's business?'
'That is one of the important things for us to discuss, but I am glad to see you got here all right. What sort of journey did you have?'
'Oh, fine. Still having trouble with deliveries?'
'Well, deliveries is another of the things we must talk about. Were you able to get anything to eat on your journey? How do you feel about some coffee?'

This is not a world shattering dialogue. It may not even seem to have great significance for the matters of moment which are to be negotiated. But if the visitor insists after this sort of dialogue in pressing his probing questions, then we start to suspect that the amber light is turning red. If he attunes to the more social wavelength, then this does not change the fact that an amber light has shone, but it does leave us with the possibility that it may yet turn green.

It is usually wrong for us at this stage to have formed a firm opinion about his orientation. We have however got these first glimmers which will usually need to be considered further as we move into the opening business phases.

Summary

What is the pattern of our behaviour to be at the outset?
1 Enter in an upright stance, expression open and friendly, shoulders relaxed, right hand unencumbered; neat, tidy and well dressed.
2 Handshake and first eye-contact conveying credibility and confidence.
3 Movement and speech setting the brisk (but not flustered) pace.
4 Discussing neutral topics.

5 Taking maybe 5 per cent of the prospective time to break the ice.

6 Standing during these opening moments (in small mixed groups if teams are negotiating).

And what shall we have achieved by doing so?

1 We shall have established an atmosphere which is cordial, based on normal social practices.

2 We shall have created a climate which has the potential for collaboration. We shall not yet have started positively to achieve the collaboration — that comes in the next stage (the opening formalities) but we shall have avoided the hostility and defensiveness which might mar subsequent collaboration.

3 We shall have established a pace of movement and discussion which is brisk and ripe for reinforcement.

4 We shall not yet have established the businesslike character. This again must wait until the opening formalities. But we shall not have pitched ourselves prematurely into contentious issues.

We shall have achieved much of our climate of cordiality and briskness; we shall need to do more work towards collaboration and towards the businesslike atmosphere.

2 The opening process

Aiming towards agreement, the Parties have (we hope) established a cordial yet brisk atmosphere, and have provided fertile ground for businesslike development of the negotiation. What now?

We move immediately into another influential stage of the negotiation. The pattern and possibilities for the negotiating process will quickly become determined, either explicitly or by the precedents which are established in this important period.

To take advantage of the opportunities for creative negotiations, we need to clear our thinking about:

- why is this period so influential?
- what should we aim to achieve?
- how?
- who leads?

Why is the period influential?

The period is influential first, because energy and concentration are naturally at a high point at the start of any activity.

At the start of a meeting there is a short period during which everybody is concentrating, and during which there is a similar pattern to what each hears and understands.

This pattern of sharp energy and concentration quickly deteriorates. Concentration lessens; within a couple of minutes of sitting down together people's attention starts to wander and they begin to hear different messages in what is being said and even to fail to hear some important statements. But for a short and influential period, we can expect high concentration.

The opening period is important second because the opening topic becomes established. The choice of opening topic, and of the form in which it is discussed, sets a precedent for the way in which subsequent topics will be approached and tackled; and so the pattern of the negotiation becomes set in the opening minute or two. Once established, the pattern is difficult to change; and at this stage, it is all too easy for the choice of topic to create the conditions for a later battle between the parties.

The period is important third, because attitudes are being formed. Each party is reading signals from what the other says and does, making continued judgements about the other's character, and framing its own behaviour in response. People at this stage are for example alert for anything which can be interpreted as aggressive and often ready themselves to become defensive and counter-aggressive.

Fourth, 'pecking order' is established. The hens in the barnyard have amongst themselves a recognised priority as to which hen is the first to peck at the corn. We are not clear about how that pecking order is established but we are clear that all hens recognise it and follow it.

People are not hens, but people are sensitive about pecking orders, and particularly sensitive about the pecking order established at the outset of important negotiations.

There are, then, good reasons to recognise that there will be a highly influential period when the negotiators first get down to business. The skilled negotiator needs to take advantage of this important period. He needs to approach it well knowing his objectives and his methods for the period.

Objectives in the opening process

At this stage of most negotiations, and at this stage of this book, our objectives are Towards Agreement. Our present concern is to start moving together in a direction which will be to our best joint advantage.

We start with a brisk and cordial atmosphere, and we now need to establish:

- a businesslike approach
- a meeting of minds as we move towards the core of our negotiations
- an early establishment of co-operation between the parties
- a shared understanding of the sequence of activity which we can both anticipate
- continuity and development of the brisk pace already established.

Method in the opening process

To get a clear picture of how to operate at this point, it is necessary here to distinguish three different dimensions of negotiating. They are:

1 the content
2 the procedures
3 the personal interaction.

Content is the range of topics to be settled. Negotiating an oil contract, the content will focus on issues such as quality of oil, quantity, delivery, terms, discounts, etc. In a banking negotiation, the content will be concerned with money, at what rates, for how long, security and repayment. The content of an engineering negotiation, with specification, inspection, control, price, delivery, terms, etc. In a labour negotiation, with terms of employment, pay and other rewards.

By *procedure* we mean the planning, agenda formulation, control of meetings, the preparation both of the physical setting and the matters to be negotiated, the preliminaries between the parties, and the pacing.

By *personal interaction* we mean the manner in which individuals involved in negotiating interact with one another. The way in which their personalities combine or conflict. The manner in which they bring influence to the negotiating table and the reactions of the Other Party to that influence. Both individually and as teams.

Negotiators coming together need first to adjust to one another as people and second to adopt some procedure to handle the matters between them. They are uncertain and insecure if they launch into discussions of the opening issues without some framework of thinking about what they hope to achieve and how.

Using the terms described above, our first concern was in the dimension of personal interaction; we set out to get the *climate* right. We now need to work on the *procedures* we will follow, before we get into the *content* issue.

We have been standing up. To emphasise the change of mood from personal to businesslike, we move to our seats from the opening ice-breaking situation. Immediately, our actions can confirm the brisk pace we are aiming for. There is a short period (maybe ten seconds) during which people are sitting down and adjusting their papers – this is a necessary brief interval before they can tune in to the new business dimension – but there must be no long gap or hesitation before the first comment is made. This detail of timing has its influence on the pace which will be sustained through the rest of the meeting.

So has the pace at which first speaker speaks, and the pace at which responder comes in and makes his opening comment.

The things which are said need to make positive use of the opportunities that exist briefly. No lo..ger is the time appropriate for the cordial chatter of the ice-breaking period – indeed, that would be a sad waste of the possibilities. The need now is to form a shared consciousness of where we are going, and how we are going to get there together.

What then should we focus on? There are four topics which we should regularly cover at this stage. They can be conveniently remembered as 'the four P's: Purpose, Plan, Pace, Personalities.

The *purpose* is the reason for our having come together. It may for example be any one or more of the following:

1 Exploratory. Seeing where one another's interests lie.
2 Creative. Aiming to identify a mutually profitable possibility.
3 Submitting evidence, or clarifying evidence, (e.g. questions previously submitted).
4 Agreement in principle.
5 Agreement on specific details.
6 Ratifying an agreement already negotiated.
7 Reviewing progress and plans.
8 Settling a dispute.

The *plan* is the agenda for the meeting. The topics to be discussed, and the order in which the parties will take them.

The *pace* is the rate at which the parties need to move — the length of time which they anticipate or are prepared to devote to the meeting.

The *personalities* are the people in each team — who they are, what they do, and what they can do of significance to the meeting.

These 'four P's' — particularly the first three, the purpose, plan and pace for the negotiation — are matters we must have prepared effectively before the meeting. (We shall be covering preparation fully in chapter 7.)

Introducing the process

The four P's are the topics to be covered during the first few moments. The manner in which we introduce them is very important.

The skill lies in immediately creating a sense of agreement, and in regularly nurturing that sense of agreement.

Again, the practice is a simple one. It is to introduce the word 'agree', in a context in which Other Party almost certainly *will* agree. For example:

'Can we first agree on procedure? I'd like to check with you on what we're hoping to achieve this afternoon, and how we should go about it. Is that agreeable to you?'

Immediately, we have injected the sense that the meeting is about agreeing, and have posed a question which begs the answer 'Yes — I agree'.

Now we need both to establish the procedure and to nurture the sense of agreement. It can be done by such a dialogue as the following:

'Well, we see the purpose of this meeting as being purely exploratory — just to exchange information on our respective positions. Is that how you see the purpose?'
'We'd like to exchange information and get one step further. We'd like to have some discussion about the area in which we might do business together.'
'Yes, we'd be glad to do that if there is time. I've assumed that this meeting will take about an hour. Is that all right for you?'
'Fine.'
'Well O.K., should we agree to spend about forty minutes exploring our respective situations? Then another twenty minutes on the joint opportunities?'

and so on — agreeing on the opening procedure to be followed; agreeing on the Purpose, on the Pace, on the Plan. Agreeing as a rule, that the first item of the plan shall handle the fourth P — the Personalities — each of us briefly to describe our role and relevant interests.

But before the 'personalities' issue, feed back and reinforce the sense of agreement.

'O.K. then, we're agreed on the purpose of this meeting and the pace at which we need to work, and the way we're going to tackle it.
And we agreed that the first item should be to introduce ourselves. Would you like me to start?'

In this way, we get the negotiation moving cordially and collaboratively, using our fourth P— Personalities (self introductions) — as a bridge towards the substantive item we have *agreed* to be first.

Who leads?

People are sensitive about power, and negotiators are often sensitive about the 'pecking order' in the opening moments. The matters at stake at this stage are:

Who is going to speak first?
Who is going to take the lead in forming the agenda?
How is the time to be distributed between the two parties?

Suggested guidelines for handling these matters are:

1 Share the dialogue. Aim for the amounts of talking time and listening time to be equally shared — at least until we have agreed on a procedure which needs one or other party to lead.
2 Brief question and statement. Let the opening procedures and discussion take place in a series of short interacting statements; not in a sequence of lengthy submissions from each party.
3 Be supportive. Offer ample opportunity for Others to make comments, take initiative. As far as possible, do so by offering questions leading to assent; and repeatedly emphasise the development of agreement.
4 Be agreeable. Wherever reasonably possible during the opening procedure, assent to his suggestions. To assent is usually more productive than to assert a conflicting viewpoint.

Subject to these guidelines being followed, the concerns about 'pecking order' can quickly be reduced.

But at the outset, when we first sit down, there is need for the meeting to get off to a brisk start. It certainly won't do so if each party sits and waits deferentially for the other to peck first, and there is need therefore for somebody to take the lead.

Unless the visitors quickly offer a lead, it is the duty of the host to make the opening suggestion — 'Can we first agree on procedure........?'

Using the process

The suggested opening is to get agreement covering Purpose,
Plan and Pace and presentation of Personalities. Under what
circumstances should we use this approach?

Almost always.

Even when the groundwork has been covered in preliminary correspondence, it is still important that both
parties share the same thoughts about purpose, plan and pace.
It is important to get these procedural aspects out of the files
and back into everyone's consciousness. And important to
emphasise from the outset that we are working together in
a spirit of *agreement.*

This applies even when one party is pushing for a different
start. It often happens that one party enters the negotiation
bursting with enthusiasm to tackle one particular issue. By
all means, let them tackle that issue – but only after we have
together agreed why we are meeting, and how we are going
to operate together.

The skilled negotiator is not reluctant to interrupt in order
to get the opening agreement on procedure. If, as we sit
down, Others start immediately on substantive issues –
'We've been looking at the issues of price, and we want to
make a few....' – then the probability is that they are going
to open with some thrust, which we shall be forced to
counter. That would have us disagreeing within minutes.
Aiming towards agreement, we must prevent it.

It is essential to interrupt – 'Excuse me a moment, but
may we just agree procedure to start with? My impression is
that we are meeting now in the hopes of reaching an agreement in principle. Is that how you see this meeting?' And
so on – insisting on establishing the four P's of the opening
process; and on establishing the practice of agreement.

Another check on strategy

At this stage, we need again to check on the strategy we are
following. Our aim is a collaborative negotiation, and our
approach is designed to move forward that way.

The opening process will have given us a new opportunity to check whether Others are interested in collaboration or not. At the same time, we shall have given them rich opportunities to see and to appreciate that our intentions are collaborative.

From their behaviour, we see new signals about their intentions. If they refuse to co-operate in setting up the procedure for the meeting, then they force us to assume that they will not co-operate in the content of the negotiation. These people are looking only to their own advantage, and we need to adopt a counter-strategy. We need to switch off from our approach towards agreement, and to start to earn counter-advantages.

But Others are unlikely to show such gross signals of conflict. They may find difficulty in joining in with our constructive approach — after all, many people have been brought up to believe that negotiation is a form of warfare — but this simply emphasises the need for our testing and pressing our strategy towards agreement. If we can successfully use this technique for opening the negotiation to generate co-operation, we shall have created a fresh range of opportunities for the negotiating process which is to follow.

Moreover, we have not yet reached a stage at which we are forced to choose between a co-operative strategy and an aggressive-defensive strategy. There are going to be further chances to test Other's intentions and for the moment we can usually continue to reserve judgement.

Rarely, then, shall we be convinced that Other is signalling a red light to our co-operative strategy. More often, we shall be finding that he responds to our co-operative approach and begins to show some green lights. Our approach should generally continue with our strategy aiming towards agreement.

Summary

The approach suggested for our opening moves into the business content of the meeting is:

1 Make positive use of the powerful opening moments.
2 Cover the 'process' issues — why we're here, what we're going to do, how long, who we are — the four P's of Purpose, Plan, Pace and Personalities.
3 Emphasise the element of agreement from the outset.
4 Especially emphasise the agreed plan.
5 De-fuse the sensitive issue of 'pecking order' by inter-active dialogue, supporting and reasonably deferential behaviour.
6 Use this 'process' approach as a routine; and continue to use it, even when preliminary work has been done or Others rush towards a different path.

The results of following this discipline are:

1 An immediate sense of agreement and co-operation.
2 Early opportunity to get results together; to get agree-ment together.
3 Shared consciousness that we are already agreeing.
4 A common framework of thinking, a plan acting as a common frame of reference when later we go through the complexities of the negotiation.
5 Another opportunity to check that Other Party has at heart our joint interests towards agreement.
6 Further development of the climate we were anxious to create — cordial, co-operative, brisk and businesslike.

3 The fabric of a negotiation

From the stages of climate formation and of opening process, the negotiations move towards business. They are likely now to move quickly into an exciting and dramatic period, during which an enormous number of ideas and impressions come clamouring for their attention.

This wealth of activity can all too easily become a jumble. To keep control of it, and to free his mind to concentrate on the content of the negotiations, the negotiator needs a framework to assess what is going on. He needs to recognise the fabric of the negotiation.

This chapter is about that framework, that fabric.

The aim is to define some aspects of what goes on repeatedly from one negotiation to another. This definition, 'what is the fabric', will then pave the way for us in chapter 4 to handle the issue 'how to conduct negotiations'.

We shall now be examining four distinct threads in the fabric:

1 The phases of a negotiation.
2 Broad front versus deep penetration.
3 The form of confrontation.
4 Structure of concentration.

The phases of a negotiation

There are five phases through which any negotiation must proceed:

> Exploration
> Bidding
> Bargaining
> Settling
> Ratifying

In the *exploratory phase* the sorts of activities which will take place are:

— The parties form an understanding of one another's requirements.
— The parties get a joint sense of the sort of deal they might be able to make.
— The parties are hardening the attitudes which they will display to one another.
— The shape of the prospective deal is beginning to get clearer.
— Recognition is growing of the issues which will need to be settled during the bargaining process.

In the *bidding phase* one or both parties put forward their own bids or offers on each of the issues in the deal.

In the *bargaining phase* each is negotiating towards the best advantage.

As this bargaining process matures, there comes a moment when each party recognises that agreement is at hand. This starts the phase of *settling* the deal.

Finally, there is the process of *ratifying* the agreement, usually in writing; sometimes in legal detail.

The manner in which these phases of negotiations are handled varies from one negotiation to another. Often they do not follow one another in clear sequence. Sometimes the parties dodge backwards and forwards between the phases. Sometimes they will follow the sequence on one aspect of the deal and then start all over again on a second aspect.

But, for effective control of the negotiating process, the

negotiator must have at the back of his mind an awareness of the five stages: exploration; bidding; settling; bargaining and ratifying.

Broad front versus deep penetration

Negotiations can be tackled on a broad front, making some progress on all issues; then coming back to make more progress – again on all issues.

Or they can be conducted with deep penetration. Concentrate on one issue, complete discussion on that issue, before starting on the second.

In the broad front or lateral approach the sequence of events is: –

- first get the broad pattern clear overall
- then start to discuss each aspect of the broad pattern
- then go into more detail across the broad pattern.

But in a deep penetration or vertical approach the sequence is:

- start on one issue, define, dive deeply into discussion of that first issue
- then start on the second issue and dive deep
- then on the third issue
- and so on until each issue has been settled.

Consider for example a deal in which there are four main issues: price, delivery, terms and quality. Under a *lateral* approach, the issues would be identified during an exploratory stage. Each party would make some statement of its priorities among these four issues. The shape of a prospective deal involving those issues would start to become clear during the creative stage. Then each party would successively state its bid on each of the four issues. If there were a bargaining phase there would be a first round of bargaining about all four issues (price, delivery, terms, quality). Then a second round of bargaining about all four issues. If necessary, a third and so on.

But in a *vertical* style of negotiating, the process would

early focus on, e.g. price, possibly without the other issues yet having even been mentioned. There would be deep diving bidding and bargaining on that issue of price. Only after agreeing on price would the negotiators consider (say) delivery at all. Then settle the delivery negotiation before starting on terms, and so on.

To summarise, the distinction is:

— broad front or *lateral* approach: in each successive round, make progress on the whole 'broad front'.

— deep penetration or *vertical* approach: one issue at a time.

The form of confrontation

Within any negotiation there are bound to be differences of view between the parties. There are two approaches to handling those differences of view: the 'follow-my-leader' and the 'independent'.

In a *follow-my-leader* discussion one party makes a statement. The Other Party then concentrates on attacking or countering that statement.

But in an *independent* sequence, the first party makes the statement, the second party gets clarification and checks that it understands the first position; then, separately, the second party defines its own position, with first party seeking clarification.

For example, a 'follow-my-leader' dialogue may go:

'Our price for these will be £150 each.'
'£150? That seems extraordinary — far more than we could afford. How do you justify it?'
'That is the going market rate for similar items which we have been selling round the corner.'
'This is astonishing. We know that we can get competitors' things a lot cheaper. You'll have to come down.'

A corresponding independent sequence would be:

'Our price for these will be £150 each.'

'That is the price per unit, is it?'

'Yes, price per unit.'

'Is that inclusive of delivery and of tax charges?'

'Inclusive of delivery, exclusive of tax.'

'Your bid then is £150 each, delivered, tax exclusive?'

'Correct.'

'Our position on price is that we have hopes of negotiating at £120, exclusive of delivery and of tax.'

And so on. First Party has stated his position; Second Party has checked and clarified. Second Party has stated his position and it's now up to First Party to get it clear before moving on.

In practice, there is a lot of difference in results from these approaches. The follow-my-leader dialogue leads the parties to argue with one another on each issue. In contrast the independent approach enables each to recognise respective positions, and then to focus on 'what can we do about it together?'

The structure of concentration

Whenever people communicate, as they do in a negotiating meeting, there is a persistent pattern of energy and concentration.

Energy is high at the outset. There is a short period, maybe two to three minutes, during which everybody concentrates hard and their thoughts focus on similar matters. (These are the critical opening moments we have already discussed in chapter 2.)

The initial concentration soon falls off sharply. Later it continues to fall off though less sharply. This decline continues until the final stages are reached.

When everybody realises that we are reaching a conclusion, there is a sudden re-awakening of energy — but only for a very short time. Any subsequent extension of the meeting will be at a 'sub zero' level and not productive.

This shape of concentration over a period of time is shown in Figure 3.1.

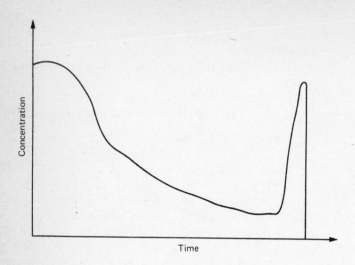

Fig. 3.1 Concentration over a period of time

Such a shape applies to the conduct of a particular meeting. If a negotiating meeting lasts one hour, then the initial high concentration level lasts for two or three minutes and the final spurt for one or two minutes only.

The same shape applies over a protracted series of meetings. For example, within a negotiation taking place over a period of six weeks, energy is high during the first half week, then declines over the next five weeks. As the parties approach the last day or two, there is a final burst of energy.

Within a particular meeting (or series), concentration does not, of course, fall as smoothly as shown in Figure 3.1. There are ripples of higher concentration, troughs of lower, as in Figure 3.2. These are critical moments at which the skilled negotiator acts in ways we shall discuss fully in chapter 4.

Within the structure of negotiation, then, concentration is high at the outset, high at the end. Positive steps are needed to capitalise on the high energy periods, and to cope with normal declines.

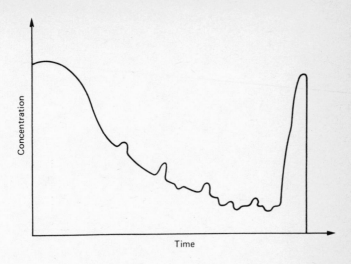

Figure 3.2 Ripples and troughs of concentration

Summary

The aim of this chapter has been to identify threads in the fabric of a negotiation, so that in the next chapter we can discuss how to control it. We have described four threads:

1 The phases of negotiation — exploration
                                                    — bidding
                                                    — bargaining
                                                    — settling
                                                    — ratifying.
2 Lateral v. vertical sequences — lateral, the broad front
                                                    — vertical, deep diving on
                                                       each successive issue.
3 Pattern of concentration — follow-my-leader — arguing
                                                       each item as anyone makes
                                                       a point
                                                    — independent — clarifying
                                                       the difference and solving

the problem together.

4 Structure of concentration — high at start
                              — ripples and troughs in the
                                middle
                              — final spurt at the end.

4 Conducting the negotiation

Our strategy as we come together to negotiate has been directed towards eventual agreement. We have created a cordial and brisk climate; we have agreed together on the purpose, the plan and pace for our meeting; we have already established the pattern of agreeing; and we have introduced the personalities present.

Altogether, in the opening few minutes, we have established a spirit which is cordially co-operative, brisk and businesslike. Continuing our movement Towards Agreement, we now enter into the conduct of negotiation.

In this chapter, the focus is again on aspects of negotiation which we can expect to recur regularly, aspects which could happen in each successive negotiation, aspects which will be made to happen by the skilled negotiator in control of negotiations.

The plan of the chapter is to cover:

- the exploratory phase
- strategy review
- bidding and bargaining
- process control
- the human element.

The exploratory phase

This phase is always important. It is extremely important when the strategy is one of negotiating towards best joint advantage.

The main elements for each Party, at this stage and with this strategy, are:

1 Opening statements.
2 The creative phase.
3 Strategy review.
4 Issue identification.

Considering the *opening statements,* the issues are what we say, how we say it, and how we respond to the Other Party.

The content (what we say) has to present the position of each Party. It must be designed to give the Other Party a clear recognition of our view.

It needs to be tackled laterally. We need to establish the broad pattern and not to deep dive into any one aspect.

Each Party should independently make a broad statement of its own position, and give opportunity for the others to seek clarification. Then get a comparable 'broad picture' of the Other Party's position, and clarify that.

Each opening statement needs to cover:

— Our understanding. The broad area within which we believe the negotiation will take place.
— Our interests. What we would like to achieve through the negotiation.
— Our priorities. What are the most important aspects for us.
— Our contribution. The way in which we can help to our joint advantage.
— Our attitudes. The consequence of our previous dealings with Other Party; their reputation as it has come to us; any special hopes or fears which we may have for collaboration.

For example,

'Well gentlemen, we have agreed that the opening step

should be for us as the users to tell you our position about the deal.

We are interested in buying the site of the property with a view to demolishing it and to building a number of shops on it. We have contacted the Planning Authorities and believe that they will accept our plans. Our key interest is timing – it is imperative for us to reach a very quick decision on this issue and, to that end, we are prepared to take steps which would hasten the normal legal and survey procedures. We have not had previous dealings with you, but our friends tell us that you are good people to deal with. That's how we see the position – is it clear?'

Characteristic of this opening statement are the following points:

1 The opening statements of each Party are independent. They state the position of our Party and do not attempt at this stage to state the joint interests of the two Parties.
2 They concentrate on the interest of our Party. They do not attempt to put our assumptions about the position of the Other Party. (The giving of this assumption serves only to irritate, to confuse and to introduce disharmony.)
3 The statements are general, not detailed. They are aiming towards a lateral and not a vertical development of the negotiation.
4 The statement needs to be brief. It should give the Other Party an opportunity to come into the discussion quickly, both so that the Parties can quickly interact and so that Others do not get a sense of being overwhelmed by either the duration or the complexity of our opening statement. Keep it short.

The method (how we say it) should reinforce the climate already developed. We are putting forward a simple business-like statement, in a way which needs to be cordial and brisk. The final words (in the example above, 'is it clear?') need particularly to be pitched to show that the statement is intended as a search for clarity and not as a challenge to opposition. Keep it friendly.

Our response to Other's opening statement needs to be in two stages:

1 Listen, clarify and summarise.
2 Offer own opening statement.

Listen. Do not waste energy by thinking up counter-arguments.
Clarify. If in any doubt, question to get clear what he is trying to say.
Summarise. Feed back the key points of what you understand him to be saying. ('O.K. − so you want to move quickly towards demolition and rebuilding?')

And when satisfied that we understand their position, confirm the procedure we agreed to follow and make our own opening statement, taking care to state our position *in*dependently, not *inter*dependently:

'Right then, we agreed that the next step should be for us to tell you our position. Shall I go on to that now?
Our position is that we are interested in selling this site. We have some degree of commitment towards retaining the present buildings on it but this is not over-riding. We are concerned to get the best possible price and have no urgency about the matter. That's how we see it − any questions you'd like to ask for clarification?'

In making their opening statements in this pattern, the Parties have continued along agreement oriented lines. They have followed an agreed procedure to the point at which they should have agreed to look together at the creative possibilities.

They now reach the stage at which agreement oriented negotiators have a unique opportunity to get something to joint advantage − something bigger than either party could get if negotiating to independent advantage. This is the moment to be seeking together to make the biggest and best cake.

In order to achieve that creativity, we need first to be imaginative. Later we shall have to impose the forces of reality, but there will rarely be anything worth imposing them on unless we first think creatively and imaginatively.

We start with the spirit of co-operation so carefully developed, and with the independent position of each Party established. We now need a statement which will both give our thoughts an impetus in the right direction, and at the same time reduce concern about being imaginative.

> 'O.K., that's how we stand, so can we now, as we agreed, take a look at the creative possibilities? I suggest that we let our thoughts flow freely for a few moments and then come back afterwards to see which of our joint ideas are realistic.
>
> Is that O.K.? Would you like me to keep a note of our joint ideas?'

The pattern of generating the ideas must be lateral and interactive. It must be *lateral* because immediately the Parties focus on one suggestion (either criticising or exploring it in depth), their minds cannot revert to broad and imaginative thinking. It must be *interdependent*, not only to sustain the co-operation between them, but also because each fresh suggestion from one Party can kindle a new ember in the imagination of the other. The Parties have great potential to be creative *together*.

> 'O.K. What ideas have we got?'
> 'Maybe there is some way we can balance the pricing issue against the delivery issue.'
> 'Payment terms, used as a bridge between us.'
> 'Seller financing buyer's next use of the land.'
> 'Tying in this deal, and the timing of it, with another deal on a different site.'
> And so on.

In this sequence, each Party's imagination is receiving stimulus from the successuve statement of the Other Party. Together they are creating a panorama of possibilities.

Contrast the collapse of creativity when Parties start deep diving:

> 'O.K. what ideas have we got?'
> 'Maybe there is some way we can balance the pricing issue against the delivery issue.'

'You mean, that we should pay more to get quick delivery?'

This dialogue is already moving the Parties into bidding and bargaining phases, without having made use of the carefully developed opportunity for creativity.

The need is therefore to develop ideas imaginatively together. This process of recognising creative possibilities should generate a number of different ideas. There then comes the need to form a bridge between the world in which the parties have been thinking imaginatively, and the world of reality in which their performance must be measured by business criteria. They must decide which of their imaginative ideas offer realistic possibilities.

They need to go through their list, and to put some evaluation on each possibility.

'Should we now take a look to see which of the possibilities are attractive?'
'Right. Well, the first was balancing price against delivery. That seems to me to be a fallback if we can't find anything better. I'd rate it B.'
'Agreed. I'm more interested in the way we might use payment terms as a bridge. Can we call that an A? We can? And what about seller financing buyer?'
'No – I'm not at all interested in that – it's a C.'

Note that neither Party should now defend the ideas it has suggested. Indeed, we agreed so when we said, 'Let our thoughts flow freely, and come back afterwards to see which ideas are realistic.'

Through such a process of opening statements, imaginative development and realistic prioritising, the exploratory phase moves forward constructively. But before we get any deeper, we need to review our strategy of 'collaboration towards agreement in our joint interests.'

Strategy review

This is the last moment to check our strategy before becoming embroiled in the central heart of the negotiating process. And in that central heart, our behaviour would need to change radically if the Other Party were not responding collaboratively. If he is fighting it, or simply assenting to it without contributing, there is a danger that he will hereafter seek simply to exploit us.

How do we go about the strategy review?

By this stage of the negotiation, the signals are usually showing very clearly. We may be seeing a clear green light: the Other Party may have joined with us through the ice-breaking period, the opening process, and the exploratory phase in so clear a manner that we have no cause for concern.

Or the Other Party may have resisted or come along with us in such a weak manner – despite our regular and repeated efforts to give every opportunity for collaboration – that we clearly see a red light: we see that he is going to take every possible step to gain independent advantage.

Usually, the light will be clearly green or clearly red; but sometimes the light may still look to be amber and we must pause to interpret. This is a convenient moment to take a break. Either to take a recess of a few minutes within a one-meeting negotiation or to break between successive sessions of protracted negotiations. During the break, we need to review the situation and to review his behaviour.

When we review the situation, we must consider: Is the nature of the deal and of his strength within it such that an aggressive strategy would be sensible for him? We may even need systematically to analyse the considerations which should be governing his strategy – considerations to be discussed fully in chapter 16.

And we need to review Other Party's behaviour:

1 What is their track record? Do they normally behave aggressively or co-operatively?
2 What evidence can be deduced from the way they behaved in the first minute or two? How far were they pressing us before we got properly started?
3 How effectively did they join in the opening process? Did they take the initiative towards a co-operative

opening? Or did they resist and maybe push in other directions?

4 Have they been open with us in defining their starting position?

5 Have they sought to exploit us at the time we defined our opening position?

6 What is the ratio of the constructive initiatives they have put into the negotiations, to the number they have taken out? And the ratio of information put in to information taken out?

From such strands of evidence, we must make up our minds whether to continue our strategy — 'Towards Agreement'; or whether now we have to change to a quite different world of competition with the Other Party.

For the time being, this book proceeds on the assumption that our strategy sensibly remains 'Towards Agreement'. We are not yet concerned with the skills of handling combative negotiations.

Rounding off the exploratory phase

After our strategy review, we have one more step to take in the exploratory phase of the negotiation: we have to *identify the issues* which will need to be discussed during the bidding and bargaining phases.

Assuming that we are co-operating 'Towards Agreement', this is simply a question of the Parties stating what they think the important issues will turn out to be. It will be one step in a *lateral* sequence of negotiating:

'All right gentlemen, it seems to me now that the issues we need to settle will be the price of the site, timing of the deal, timing of payment, the financing, and the legal charges. Does that cover the issues you would like resolved?'

To summarise:

The exploratory phase in a co-operative negotiation includes opening statements which are independent and which are checked for clarity but not for argument.

As these independent statements have been made and acknowledged, the Parties have an opportunity to look imaginatively for creative possibilities.

We are then wise to check that our strategy 'Towards Agreement' is still promising.

At the end of the exploratory phase we should identify the issues for the next phase.

Bidding and bargaining 'Towards Agreement'

Ideally, this bidding and bargaining pattern should have the characteristics:

1 Sequence, lateral: the broad front approach.
2 Confrontation of position and not confrontation with 'opponent'.
3 Consistent use of joint problem solving.
4 Recycling: each successive lateral stage containing new elements of exploration and creativity.

At the opening of the phase, with the range of issues having already been identified, First Party needs to define where it stands on that range of issues.

'Looking at that range of issues, we are advised that we can sell at a price of up to £200,000. The timing is not of concern to us, within the six months or so.
Our best advantage would be for full payment at an early stage and.........'

The Second Party needs to check on these issues for clarification.
For example:

'When you say 'up to £200,000' I understand that to be a maximum you could expect. Is that correct?'

As long as we are following this strategy, it is important to avoid the corresponding aggressive questions. ('Well, if what you are expecting is a maximum of £200,000, what do you think would be a fair settlement area?') Aggressive questions demand counter-aggressive answers and lead towards warfare.

Having obtained the clarification it needs, Second Party defines own position and First Party gets clarification.

> 'Well, our situation is that this is one of four sites, any one of which might be of interest to us. Our thinking on price is that we would be very interested at . . . . . .'

Now, together, the Parties need to identify the areas of overlap in their bids, and the problem areas they must together resolve.

It is helpful at this stage to focus on agreement, not to focus on disagreement.

NOT 'Well thank you for telling me, but we'll have to ask you to look again at price and delivery.'

BUT RATHER 'Thank you for that explanation. It seems to me that we can readily agree on finance, agree on terms, and agree on legal charges. The problems concerning us are only in the areas of price and delivery. Is that how you see it?'

Note that the form of the last question, virtually demanding a 'yes' answer, is again serving to stress the positive agreement between the Parties.

This does not of course camouflage the fact that there are real differences between the positions of the two. But it does clarify where the differences are. It sets them in a context of agreement. It creates an appreciation from which the Parties can go forward together creatively to solving the problem.

This may be the time for a recess or alternatively it may be an opportunity for the Parties again to ask whether they can see creative approaches to solving the problem newly identified.

The process of bidding and bargaining laterally in this manner is one of successive moves on a broad front. At each stage, the broad problem is examined. The possibilities are kept open of trading one item against another, without the deep diving and in-fighting of competing on each issue separately.

To summarise:

When the negotiation strategy is 'Towards Agreement', then the bidding and bargaining needs to be a co-operative process. Not a fight.

The sequence needs to be of a succession of advances on a broad front. First towards agreement in principle, then agreement on broad detail, then agreement on the final detail.

The dialogue needs to define respective positions and to get them clarified. Not to treat one another's positions as points for attack.

The parties are moving forward together, recognising what they have in common, recognising what they have both achieved, together confronting the problems that face them.

Not confronting one another.

Process control

The skilled negotiator, working Towards Agreement, is of course heavily involved in the content of what is being negotiated. But much of his influence lies in his ability to keep simultaneous control of the process of negotiating; he needs control of how they're doing it.

Process control skills are not always obvious. It may be that one member of the team is seen to have little impact whist his colleagues are toughly bargaining over price and delivery. Yet often such a member has an unnoticed but massive influence through occasional interjections. For example, while the price/discount debate seems to be moving to an impasse, the whole direction of a negotiation can be changed by the quiet man saying 'Would it help us to look at terms of payment at this stage?'

That is an example of a procedural intervention by the quiet man. Within any group there always seems to be one person who has a natural talent to make that sort of intervention. Such natural talents are influential, often beyond the recognition of colleagues.

They are talents which create ripples in concentration during the negotiation.

What then are the steps the negotiator can take to control
the process of the meeting?

1 Summarising. Helping the parties together to recognise
where they've got to in the content of the negotiation.
2 Clarifying the situation. Encouraging them to clear their
minds on 'what we're talking about' and 'what's the
problem'.
3 Clarifying the process. Using his insight into 'broad front
v. deep-penetration' or into 'follow-my-leader v. independent', to help the parties together to move
forward. For example:

> 'It seems to me that we have now spent as much time
> as we should for the present in delving into the issue
> of (delivery), and that we should now take a broad
> look at the other issues. Can we start talking about
> . . . . . .?'

> or

> 'Well, I feel we've now gone a long way to giving you
> our views on the issues, and I'd now like to know
> your views.'

4 Progress review. It is, of course, most influential when
progress can be checked against a standard agreed
between the Parties — most influential when it is
checked against the Purpose, Pace and Plan agreed in
the opening process of the meeting.
5 Bridging. Finding a way of building a bridge between
the parties, so that they can meet and move on
together. There is an example above, in the quiet man
introducing terms of payment as a bridge in a price/
discount argument.
6 Emphasising agreement. Using and repeating references
to the fact that we are people who agree with one
another. Reminding us when we're wandering around
during item 2 on our agenda, of the purpose that we
agreed for the meeting: reminding us of the Plan we
agreed; reminding us of the Pace we *agreed;* reminding
us of what we *agreed* in discussion of item 1 of our
plan; reminding us of what we *agreed* to do on item
2; getting us to *agree* on how we continue item 2.

These are all means to cause positive ripples in the concentration and development of a negotiation. The skilled negotiator is also alive to the likelihood of troughs.

He knows that troughs become more likely as time goes by; and he tries to pace each session so that it will finish before the troughs appear. But he knows that inevitably they will sometimes happen, and he is sensitive to them. He recognises them immediately — without being fully conscious of it, he's been influenced by changes in the speed at which people are talking, the way they are sitting, the look in their eyes, the way they're comprehending one another.

What does he do? He proposes a recess. He firmly suggests a break (so giving everyone that short burst of concentration which comes at the end of a session), quickly summarising where we're at, suggesting when to meet again, and what next steps we need to help us move forward in the agreed direction.

This tactical use of recesses is so influential a tool that we shall come back to it as a special item in chapter 5.

There is, then, a great deal of skill in controlling the process of negotiating: skill in creating ripples, skill in preventing troughs, skill in helping the parties to move forward together Towards Agreement.

The human element

The conduct of negotiations is influenced not only by the real situation in which the two Parties find themselves. It is influenced also by the way in which the Parties react to one another on a human level.

Important aspects of this interaction are:

> Pecking order
> Trust
> Physical sustenance
> Humour.

The *pecking order* covers such issues as who pecks first, who pecks most, who pecks loudest, who has most control.

For full collaboration between Parties, there must be no undue signs of either party dominating the other.

The development of *trust* is a more complicated problem.

The opening moves should have established the cordial qualities of the negotiation; but collaboration depends both on the cordial atmosphere and on this element of trust.

It is in the nature of human beings that there can never be total trust between them. There is always some element of doubt, however small or large. The prudent negotiator requires that the Other Party should earn the benefit of that doubt; but he need not hold back in giving them the chance to earn it. Indeed, he can often encourage them to do so.

The elements to earn this benefit are:

1 Openness.
2 Credibility.
3 Integrity.

The openness relates to the way in which he is prepared to offer procedures, information, and contributions which are to the common benefit. If he is consistently 'holding his cards to his chest', holding back information, demanding more than he gives, pressing towards personal advantage — then he is not interested in the creative possibilities of collaboration.

Openness includes personal frankness as well as business frankness. It includes the readiness to reveal one's own feelings and hopes and fears, as well as to be open with statements about business situations and objectives.

Openness of course may be dangerous. It might give advantage to unscrupulous opponents, and it is imperative that the agreement oriented negotiator should check on his strategy — be sure that Others are playing the game according to the same rules — not give away vast areas of advantage until he has established the Other's willingness to collaborate.

But at the same time, the greater the extent to which he can be open, step by step, the greater is his chance of inducing the Other Party to act in a like manner. When I am a member of international negotiating teams, I am constantly astonished by the length to which some of my collaborative colleagues are prepared to go in this openness and, almost as often, astonished at the collaborative response which they get from Others.

Openness alone is not enough. There must also be credibility. Each statement made by either Party must be credible. The most extreme example is in the making of bids or offers during negotiations, when a Party who makes an extravagant bid — one which he cannot justify — immediately loses credibility.

The development of trust stretches beyond the confines of the negotiating room. The integrity is seen in the spirit — not only in the letter — in which each party sets out to implement the agreements which have been negotiated between them. This understanding of integrity spills over from one round of negotiations to another and becomes a key part of the goodwill between parties.

But there are also steps towards proving integrity which may be taken at the negotiating table. For example, in my own contacts with clients, I am quite prepared to talk about what another client has required, or to talk about who an existing client may be. But I am not prepared to do both: I am not prepared both to identify a client and to describe his particular interests. When another client is faced with this blank refusal to discuss the combination of 'who and what', his immediate reaction may be negative, but there is long term gain: he now becomes confident that his own affairs will not be discussed publicly with other people and, I trust, he gains a new respect for my integrity.

Collaboration then rests not only on the mood established in the opening minutes but in the development of trust based on openness, credibility and integrity, throughout and beyond the negotiating process.

Negotiators need *physical sustenance:* food — fresh air — reasonable temperature — and a supply of coffee or other refreshment. It is a duty of the host to provide them.

And negotiations need *humour.* A few light touches can turn a hard and difficult negotiation into an enjoyable experience. Occasional smiles, occasional light laughter can make the difference between a cloudy protracted period of negotiations, and a bright and satisfying agreement achieved by collaborative negotiators.

Summary

After building the foundations for our negotiation in the ice-breaking and opening process stages, we should:

1 Give our general views on the broad field to be covered.
2 Obtain a briefing on Other Party's view.
3 Look together at the possibilities for joint advantage.
4 Check validity of our strategy 'Towards Agreement'.
5 Sustain a lateral negotiating sequence — successive moves on a broad front.
6 Emphasise areas of agreement.
7 Work together with Other Party on problem areas.
8 Control the negotiating process, against the agreed plan.
9 Develop our personal relationships and earn the other man's trust.

By following these guidelines we will achieve:

1 Best prospect of agreement.
2 Strong chance of together improving 'the size of the cake'.
3 Goodwill.
4 Brisk and businesslike negotiations.

5 Tactics 'Towards Agreement'

Tactics... counter-tactics... manoeuvres... ploys. These are words which describe devices used occasionally during negotiations. Generally, such devices are used to gain special advantage for one's own Party, but there are some which are aids to collaboration towards joint agreement.

In this chapter, we concentrate on such agreement oriented tactics. The plan is to review eight of them:

1 Recessing.
2 Setting deadlines.
3 'What if...?'
4 Full disclosure.
5 'All I've got is 60 per cent.
6 Lubrication.
7 The Golf Club.
8 Study group.

Recessing

Taking a break of five or ten minutes during which each Party moves out of the negotiating forum to reconsider the progress of the negotiation, and to reconsider its own position; or breaking off until a later session.

Usually, Other Party's response is appreciative. Skilled negotiators will recognise the benefit not only to themselves but also to the Other Party and to their mutual co-operation.

The implications for the negotiations are positive — parties have the opportunity to consolidate, to review and to recalculate, possibly to consider new initiatives or a positive re-shaping of a prospective deal and to come together again in a new atmosphere. Moreover, energy and concentration are regenerated.

On the negative side, the disadvantages might be thought to include a loss of momentum, disturbance of an effective climate and the chance for the Other Party to consult negatively. But in practice, these fears are rarely justified.

Recessing is such an important device that the method of using it deserves to be examined. When do we use it? How do we arrange it? How do we re-start after it?

First, at what times should we use our recess?

At the end of a phase in the negotiations.

That is, (a) when exploration is completed, before the start of the bidding; (b) after bids have been tabled, before getting down to bargaining and (c) possibly, depending on the momentum of the negotiations at that time, as the shape of settlement becomes clear.

Before issue identification.

We have strongly advocated opening negotiations in a manner designed to breed co-operation to mutual advantage; but we have said that this strategy needs to be checked before becoming too deeply embroiled. If in doubt, take a recess.

When nearing an impasse.

If it seems that negotiations are coming to the point at which one or another issue is a stumbling block — then it is wise to recess before the Parties become too hard in their attitudes — too committed to positions they would be forced to defend.

And, as long as we aim 'Towards Agreement', such a recess can be used to look for means together to tackle the problem which is facing the parties in their negotiation.

Under these conditions, great advantage can be gained from using the recess not for the Parties to separate but for the Parties to mix. Sub-groups of technical people from either side, and of commercial people, and of financial people — each aiming to obtain some constructive move for the negotiations as a whole.

Team maintenance needs.

When the members of the Party need to review their effectiveness as a team.

Breaking a trough.

When concentration has lapsed and needs regenerating.

Second, what is the recommended procedure to get a recess?

1 State the need for a recess — 'I think it would help our joint progress if we took a short recess now . . .'
2 Summarise and look forward — 'We're seeking to find ways to agree on the price/discount issues, and I suggest that we both look to see if we can see new ways of coping...'
3 Agree duration — '... Would fifteen minutes be agreeable?'
4 Avoid fresh issues — If Others want to insert anything further, ask them to wait until after the recess. Don't go beyond the brief spurt of energy with which people respond to the prospect of a break.

During the recess, the main items for consideration by Our Party will be obvious; discussions about how to handle the next stage, calculations on matters we have been discussing, reviews of Our Team's performance, or fresh plans for the rest of the negotiation. But, at the same time, we need to remember and to prepare for the re-opening of the negotiations, considering Plan and Re-opening Statement. Ideally, with new initiatives towards agreement.

Third, after the recess, we need to re-open with a

miniature version of the steps we always take to open a negotiation.

1 A few moments of ice-breaking, as we again attune our wavelengths.
2 Re-state agreed progress on agreed plan.
3 Confirm rest of agreed plan or suggest/agree changes to it.
4 Re-opening statements, defining positions and interests as they are now perceived; and paving the way to further creative development.

Recessing is potentially a very influential device. Disciplined use can make it a device helping us towards profitable co-operation.

Setting deadlines

Defining the time by which a negotiation meeting must have finished ('I am booked on the 11.30 plane'); or the deadline for a series of negotiations ('I am instructed to offer this to the Ethiopians if we cannot agree before 14 March').

Other Party reaction depends on the way in which the deadline is imposed. Unilateral statements (such as those quoted above) are seen as threats. They cause resentment and counter-aggression. As such they are part of the armoury of the effective fighting negotiator.

If however the deadline is one which is agreed between the two parties (not simply imposed by one of them) then the atmosphere becomes more collaborative. Contrast the first quotation above and the alternative.

'It would be a great help to me if we were able to conclude this meeting in time to catch the 11.30 plane. Would it be all right with you if we aim to move at that speed?'

The implications for the negotiation of having a deadline are positive. The pattern which negotiations follow is one we have previously described; short period of high energy; continuous decline; final burst of energy. The deadline leads to minds concentrating on creative solutions and on constructive compromise. Absence of a reasonable deadline leads to parties dragging out arguments to the further depths, without counter-balancing gains.

The setting of a deadline thus helps to concentrate the mind, the energy, the effort, the speed of achievement.

There is however a negative influence if either Party feels too early a deadline has been imposed. The counter is simple — say 'No'.

'What if...?'

The tactic of keeping the shape of a deal fluid. Constantly coming in with such questions as 'What would happen to the price if we doubled the order?' 'What change could you make in specification if we did the quality control ourselves?'

This is a constructive tactic when used during the exploratory and creative phases of a negotiation. The purpose is then to help the Parties together to identify the best shape of deal to their mutual advantage.

The same tactic however becomes disruptive if used when Parties have advanced far into the negotiating process. If there has been a great deal of work on the preparation of a bid and even further into negotiating on that bid — and Other Party then asks 'What if we [made some major change]?' — this is likely to damage the co-operation and progress towards agreement.

It is a constructive tactic when used in the phase of general exploration.

Full disclosure

Literally, this means complete readiness to give to Other Party all one's information.

In practice, total disclosure is not worth our consideration. People have neither the communicating ability nor the degrees of frankness which would be needed to make total disclosure a possibility. There will always be some elements they are unwilling and some other elements they are unable to disclose.

We therefore have to interpret 'full disclosure' as meaning the disclosure of 90 per cent of what we perceive. As such, it is the opposite of 'holding the cards close to one's chest'.

Some authorities believe that full disclosure is always suicidal during negotiations. I do not agree. It is far from 'always' suicidal.

There are some negotiators whose character is strongly inclined towards openness and frankness. They have the ability to reach out towards agreement with the Other Party; and repeatedly to offer information and creative initiative. This pattern of behaviour can be highly productive — inducing the Other Party to respond and to co-operate.

'Full disclosure' then becomes an advantage, a strength which Our Party can exploit, providing that it is used in conjunction with all the skills of negotiating 'Towards Agreement'. It is of course a fatal disadvantage when offered to Others whose sole interest lies in their own advantage, and it is thus most important that we should have reviewed our strategy before getting beyond the exploratory phase.

'All I've got is 60 per cent'

The straightforward statement that one cannot offer the full price asked, or cannot afford to wait the full delivery time.

If true, this is a constructive statement. It is an element of full disclosure and it enables the Parties together to concentrate on the problem and to search for solutions. For example, on price, they can search for alternative qualities to meet the present problem; or on delivery, they can put respective production staffs to work in a subgroup to see if they can get round the problems . . . maybe by erection in parallel with fabrication . . . or by overtime working on an existing plant . . . or by subcontracting by one or both parties etc.'

The same tactic, 'All I've got is 60 per cent...' can of course be differently used by one Party to get independent advantage, but that is another story and not yet an element under review.

Lubrication

'Bribery' is repulsive to the spirit of the Christian ethic. Legally and morally, it is outside the bounds of reasonable behaviour in most Western countries.

But in other cultures, there is nothing repulsive about lubrication of a business deal. It is the normal way of life. Without lubrication, business will not be done.

Lubrication is an art.

It may be more or less subtle. It is not necessarily the same as bribery — there are plenty of different ways of offering inducements to negotiators.

In form and extent, the pattern varies from one region to another and it needs local expertise to manage the process. Moreover, for reputable Western negotiators, the morality of lubrication tends to be a deterrent. They need to retain local agents who will handle this aspect of the negotiation process for them.

I do not like bribery. But I do recognise that in some cultures, lubrication is an essential ingredient for negotiating towards agreement, an ingredient which the skilled negotiator must provide for even when he himself is not the right person to handle it.

The Golf Club

This is a tactic used, particularly by team leaders, at times when they are dissatisfied with the rate of achievement in the negotiating forum. It is a tactic to be used at times when their respective teams are reaching stalemate and progress is interrupted.

The tactic is for the team leaders to agree to meet, informally, in some environment which encourages mutual trust and openness.

For many people that atmosphere of mutual trust and respect is found in the Golf Club. For Englishmen, it is found in the Gentlemen's Club. For Finns it is in the sauna.

This tactic has positive advantages in refreshing the co-

operative spirit between the parties, in enabling them to recognise issues in common, in providing time and opportunity
for new initiatives to develop. Its value is in lifting discussion
out of the on-going negotiation forum, into a different level
– and so it is no good doing all the negotiations in the Club!

One disadvantage is that the team leaders are seen to be
operating independently of their respective teams. Unless
there is good teamwork within the teams, then their team
spirit may suffer.

But used sparingly, it is a productive tactic.

The study group

When the negotiations between teams get bogged down, it is
then helpful to set up a sub-group. For example, when matters
are reaching an impasse over delivery, then the production
people from the suppliers can form a sub-group with one or
two members of the purchasers, with terms of reference to
find means of resolving the delivery problem to their mutual
advantage.

There are great advantages to having such study-groups.
They take an element of delay out of the continuing lateral
process of negotiation. They bring together those members
of the teams who have most at stake on the contentious
issue and, skilfully used by the respective team leaders,
the device gives those members a common focus; they need
together to achieve something on behalf of the full
committee. This can powerfully change the spirit of individuals who were previously warring in public.

At the same time, the main Parties are freed to concentrate
on other aspects of the negotiations or to give time to their
other duties.

Summary

There are some tactics which can be used by negotiators
co-operating towards mutual advantage:

1 Recessing: a profitable device for both parties.

2 Setting deadlines: helping briskness and the concentration of energy.
3 Sensitive use of full disclosure.
4 Co-operative use of 'what if' and 'all I've got' devices.
5 Lubrication: whether we like it or not, there are places
  where it's practical.
6 In team-negotiations, uses of the Golf Club and the
  study group.

6 Communications

Effective negotiation depends on effective communication.

In this chapter we shall be helping to build the skills of appreciating:

1 Differences of viewpoint in communication.
2 Barriers to communication.
3 Improving communications during negotiations.
4 'Personal impact' skills.

Differences of viewpoint in communication

Whenever two parties come together, each has in its mind a picture of the situation.

These pictures are never the same. There is always what we see (Figure 6.1). The Other Party always sees things from a

Fig. 6.1 What we see

different viewpoint (Figure 6.2).

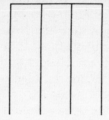

Fig. 6.2 What they see

There is some overlap between the respective views, but there is a lot which is seen only by one side, and a different lot seen only by the others (Figure 6.3).

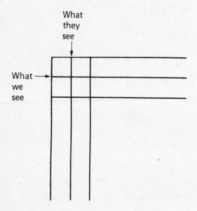

Fig. 6.3 Some overlap — plus a lot of differences of view

When two parties come together, their communications (and negotiations) are biased in this manner. They don't see the same facts, they don't interpret the facts in the same way, they don't have the same feelings.

If the parties are tense, then their concentration focuses sharply on justifying themselves. They concentrate on justifying their own position; their energy goes into thinking about their next statement; they do not listen to the Other's point of view, let alone understand or appreciate it.

Then successive statements tend towards irritating one another. Increasingly, discussion becomes controlled by those parts of the brain which are not receptive to the other side's message; and the parts which could be receptive become inactive.

There is bad communication. There is minimum overlap between the perception of the two parties (Figure 6.4).

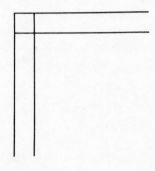

Fig. 6.4 Minimum overlap

Such a serious communications blockage can lead only towards deadlock or battle. It cannot produce any advantage to either party, unless it be the simple power-success of a strong party bullying a weaker into submission.

Strenuous communication efforts are needed if each party is to get new insight into the other's views. Then,when either party gains a bit more information, it can (because it is looking at things from a different angle) gain new insights going beyond what Other Party has just stated. In the symbolism of our diagram:

— We start with some element of overlap of views (Figure 6.5).

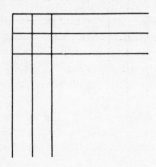

Fig. 6.5 Some overlap of views

— They manage to convey to us (and we to understand) some new item of information — like A in Figure 6.6.

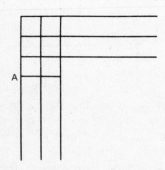

Fig. 6.6 New information heard

— We, looking from another angle, can now take a further leap forward (Figure 6.7).

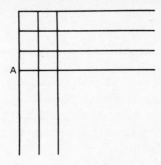

Fig. 6.7 New information enables leap forward

— As successively we are able to pass more information to them and they to us, we come to have more and more of the picture in common (Figure 6.8).

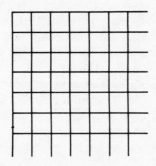

Fig. 6.8 Communication establishes condition for creative negotiations

Consider a practical example.
Richard Lucas goes to see Robert Moon, who claims that Richard's company has delivered a defective bit of equipment.

Richard goes with all the evidence which proves that the item was thoroughly tested and in good order when it was despatched.

Richard asserts all this evidence, forcefully and competently.

And Robert asserts equally forcefully and equally competently that the item broke down. He says it didn't arrive in time to be properly run in and it's all Richard's fault.

But Richard doesn't hear Robert: he's too busy arguing that there was nothing wrong with the equipment. He gets furious because Robert won't accept the simple evidence.

Robert, after trying for a little to put across his point about late delivery, finds himself forced increasingly to state and re-state, 'But it didn't work. . . but it didn't work.'

Of course, as outsiders, we know that the real problem was the late delivery, and the steps Robert should have taken to cope. But that was never diagnosed by the negotiating parties – much to the loss of their respective goodwills.

This is a trivial sounding example; yet it is taken direct from experience with very important negotiators, each used to handling contracts in millions of dollars, and each utterly astonished when they later discovered that they *hadn't heard one another.*

There are then, differences of viewpoint which must be reduced before we can communicate and negotiate to best effect. We need shortly to define practical steps which will help to make our communications effective; but first, let us look more closely at the barriers to be overcome in our communications.

Barriers to communication

In family reprimands a phrase often used is 'Did you hear what I said?' A question which often leads to puzzled silence.

In fact, hearing is not enough. Different people receive quite different messages from what any individual may say.

In a series of tests it is easy to show that less than 50 per cent of what is said is remembered in the same way by a number of listeners. Listening to one message the listeners get about one-third of the message as intended by the speaker; one-third garbled; and one-third is not heard at all. And different listeners receive different one-thirds.

In the process of communication, there are the following possible barriers:

What is spoken may not be heard.

What is heard may not be understood.

What is understood may not be accepted.

The speaker may not discover what the listener has heard/understood/accepted.

The first of those barriers is between what is *spoken* and what is *heard*. These are chiefly physical barriers: noise, lack of concentration, deafness, distortion during transmission, e.g. by telephone or microphone.

Second, whatever the listener may *hear,* what he *understands* is influenced by his education, his technical knowledge of the subject, his vocabulary; that is, by a series of intellectual abilities or barriers.

Third, whatever he may *understand,* his readiness to *accept* is influenced by psychological factors: his attitudes towards the Other Party, his attitudes towards Other Party's organisation, his feelings about the sort of package which is being discussed, his previous experience of dealing with this firm, or that product, his prejudices (even for or against dealing with men with moustaches).

Fourth, the speaker often assumes that he has been perfectly understood, and the listener is usually concerned only to make a successive statement or counter-statement; neither bothers to check on the effectiveness of their communication.

Improving communications during negotiation

Effective negotiation, depending on effective communication, must overcome the differences of viewpoint and the natural barriers in the communication process. What practical steps should negotiators take?

There are practical steps of five kinds:

1 Creating the right conditions.
2 Getting time scales right.
3 Preparing and presenting information effectively.
4 Listening effectively.
5 Overcoming 'second language' barriers.

First, the right conditions need to be established in the opening stages. This is to underline the importance of 'creating the climate'.

Second, our communications need to get the *time scale* right.

The ability to understand what is said is influenced in part by the time scale during which it is said. During a dialogue between two parties there is some time scale which is recognised as acceptable by both parties; there is a time frame which is the longest for which either party can talk without over-taxing the Other Party.

That time frame, in a *dialogue* during negotiations, is a maximum of about two minutes.

> Don't talk for more than two minutes without giving
> him a chance to interject.

There is another time frame which parties find acceptable for a monologue, i.e. for one party who has the right to present a case or statement of intent on time. This time frame is probably about five minutes.

> That is, if one party says 'Let me now tell you about the
> product. It is, etc.....', then the listener's concentration
> will be strained after about five minutes.

This time frame can be heavily influenced by the expectation which the party creates.

> If the introduction were 'Let me now tell you about the
> product. I will need about fifteen minutes to give you a
> full picture. Is that all right?' — then the listener,
> attuned to this expectation of fifteen minutes, will go
> on receiving for that period.
> Incidentally fifteen to twenty minutes is the maximum
> for this time frame, even when expectations are suitably
> created.

Another time frame is the duration through which parties can effectively sustain a dialogue, in other words, the length of a negotiating session.

This duration seems to be a maximum of about two hours. And two hours should be interrupted once or twice for recesses, to give each party a chance to reconsider and to recover concentration.

Summarising on 'timing': keep it short – maxima of two minutes for any one speaker in a dialogue; five minutes for case presentation (or fifteen to twenty if expectations suitably prepared); two hours, broken by recesses, for any one session.

Third, in these measures to improve communications during negotiating, our *presentation of information* must be effective.

This needs at the outset a desire by the speaker to put priority on to the effectiveness of communication, even at the expense of elegance. Saying it beautifully does not matter. What matters is having it understood.

To ensure the message is understood, prepared statements should be properly prepared. The method of preparation we advocate is in two stages: first a brain-storming, then a thinking stage.

In the first stage, take a clean sheet of paper, jot down a title and then – very, very quickly – a series of words, one or two words for every thought one has about the subject area.

It does not matter that this may be a jumble. It does not matter that it might include some irrelevancies. It does not matter that the thinking will not be well developed.

The purpose is rapidly to clear one's mind of the clutter which is in it.

In fact the nature of the human brain is such that it can be very fertile for a brief period – maybe a couple of minutes – in producing this range of thoughts and impressions about a subject. But if the brain tries to combine production of existing thoughts with analysis of those thoughts, then it finds itself overloaded and it becomes incapacitated. It goes round and round in circles.

It is therefore important that the negotiators specifically strive first to produce the ideas on to paper and not yet to

Cancelled Generator Contract

Finished designs	Continuous development
Nearing production	Offered discounts
Need money	Legal position?
No new orders	No concern about
Will they replace?	materials
Why did they cancel?	Harry's view ex
New business needs	production
Development possibilities	Jack's point re
A new view	Middle East
Their business situation	What on-costs?
Loss of reputation	Any creative option?
Retain goodwill	Develop some
Direct costs trivial	new generator
Maybe 100,000	together?
On-costs critical	
Overhead recovery	

Fig. 6.9 Rough ideas about the subject. (As hypothetically drafted by a supplier going to negotiate compensation, for purchaser's cancellation of a contract.)

analyse them or to be in any way self-critical. Figure 6.9
illustrates such a jumble of ideas at the start of preparations
for negotiating; the example is from negotiating compensation for a cancelled contract.

Cancelled Contract

Our hopes
            Goodwill
            New order?
            Development deal?
            Fair compensation
Key dates/value
            Date of order
            Delivery schedule
            Date of cancellation
            Price
Our situation
            Work completed
            Work-in-hand
            Materials purchased
            Dislocation
The formal position
            The contract
            Legal advisor's comment

Fig. 6.10 Plan for opening statement

At the brain-storming stage then, we take a short period of time, intensively, to clear our minds on the subject.

At the thinking stage, we should think first of the Other Party.

Sit back. Think of them. Think of their interests, their motivation, their character, their experience. Let the framework of our presentation grow out of this thinking about the Other Party.

Keep it simple. Under a simple title, set out a framework with four main headings. Four is the number which the human brain can handle comfortably: the number which the presenter can readily remember and handle, the number which the listener can readily absorb.

Then build up sub-headings under each of the four main headings — two or three supporting points or explanations under each (Figure 6.10).

Continue this part of the preparation by writing not more than four or five key words, printed large, on a postcard (Figure 6.11). This is the 'prompter' to take into the meeting. If the preparation has been so systematically done then the postcard is enough to prompt one's sub-conscious recollection

Fig. 6.11 Prompter for opening statement

during the meeting, when one's conscious energy should be directed towards the Other Party.

Finally, prepare simple visuals to support the presentation.

In the oral presentation, make use of the high concentration parts at the beginning and the end of the presentation: at the start, give Other Party a quick over-view of the main points to be made: then develop each main point: and at the end, reinforce with a summary.

Whilst presenting the case, concentrate energy on the Other Party and on their reactions. Use eyes, posture, gesture. Create visuals — figures, headlines, graphs. Wherever possible reinforce the oral word with simple figures and graphs, and even printed headlines.

Wherever possible, check — 'Can you please help me to check whether I have communicated this effectively — what were the main points which you understood me to be making?'

The third of the group of communicating skills, then, lies in the preparation and presentation of information.

Fourth, we need to be competent *listeners*. We need to make a deliberate effort to listen to and to understand the Other's perspective.

Helpful steps are:

1 Independent statements — that is, the recommended practice of getting his statement out into the open and clarified; then independently giving our statement, and ensuring that it is clear to him. Not arguing with one another.
2 Note taking — a good aid to concentration.
3 Note the speaker's non-verbal communication, and be responsive with one's own pattern of nods, expressions, gestures and eye-contact.
4 Asking questions to get clarification.
5 Feeding back our understanding of what the speaker says.

> 'Let me please summarise the key points I have understood from your statement and check that I have got them right.'
> 'I understand you to say that . . . .'

By contrast, ineffective listeners behave quite differently. Instead of concentrating on what is being said, they think about their own rebuttals or next comments. They interrupt before the speaker has completed his statement. Their responses are not questions for clarification, but counterpoints or questions which confront or contradict. They take no steps to check on the accuracy of their understanding.

Ineffective listeners then are so bound up in their own thoughts and perspectives that they have neither the time nor the inclination to get an adequate view of the Other Party's situation.

Fifth, people who have to negotiate in a *second language* often feel at a disadvantage. They believe there is a language barrier, which dominates and disrupts their communication.

I find the opposite. I find that (subject to some minimum knowledge of the second language) negotiators communicate better in the second than in their native language.

The reason seems to be that each party is constantly aware of the problems of communicating; very much more aware than negotiators both operating in their native language. Each therefore takes steps, consciously or sub-consciously, to communicate simply and effectively, to strengthen the non-verbal processes in their communication, to listen effectively, and to check on one another's understanding. Result: effective communications.

To ensure effective communication during negotiations, then, we must first have taken the trouble to prepare our information, and we must have created a good climate at the outset of the negotiation. We must then present that information effectively and must keep the different time frames in mind. We must listen effectively and make use of our opportunities if we have to negotiate in a second language.

The negotiator's personal impact

This 'personal impact' depends on the way in which he presents his views. He needs skills in the way he uses:

> his voice

his non-verbal skills
silence
visual aids.

First, the voice. It has four variables. The negotiator needs to use each at an appropriate level; and also to modulate his use of them. The variables are:

the *pace* at which he speaks
the *pitch*
the *power* or volume — and note that a change of volume can be very influential. If you really want people to listen to one passage of what you are saying, try talking very quietly rather than very loudly.
use of *pauses* — both for the speaker to think out the pattern of his next statements and to help his listeners absorb statements just made. When a speaker is sufficiently in control of his presentation, a pause of several seconds can be both helpful and very influential.

The second group of personal impact skills is the non-verbal skills.

The most powerful of these is the use of eye-contact (see reference 1).

There is some pattern of eye-contact which is intuitively recognised by people as necessary and desirable to their relationship. Researches have shown that this need can be very clearly defined both in terms of the frequency of contact and of the duration of each contact. It may be for negotiators, a norm of say six to eight eyeball-to-eyeball contacts, each of about three-fifths of a second during any minute. Too much eye-contact — either too many contacts or too long — becomes positively embarrassing for both parties. Too little reduces the influence of the negotiator and the effectiveness of communication between the two parties.

The negotiator should, as far as possible, keep free of the distraction of detailed papers in front of him. He cannot at the same time use his eyes to look at detailed papers, and use them to influence the Other Party. (And there are times when he needs his eyes, not only for contact, but also for observation — what Others are seen to be doing can occasionally give a better idea of their thoughts, than what they are saying.)

He needs to keep his eyes free from distracting papers; but he still needs some guidelines to keep him conscious of what he is trying to do in the *melée* of negotiating. He needs to have visible the headlines of the plan being followed, or of the opening statement he is making, or a few essential figures he can quote. It is for this reason that we have advocated that the final stage of preparation should be — postcard, printed large, where one glance of the eye serves as a sufficient prompt for the sub-conscious.

In addition to this very important element of eye-contact, forms of non-verbal contact include posture, gesture and expression. An alert posture has one sort of influence on Other Party and on the pace of the meeting. Quite a different influence comes from a slouching position, body slumped and one arm hanging limply over the back of the chair.

Gestures, particularly by the use of hands, are an expressive additional influence. They can reinforce a verbal message, help to retain Other's concentration, and add zest and energy to the proceedings. Or, used excessively, they can become disruptive.

Facial expressions can convey pleasure, friendship, happiness, surprise, fear, suffering, anger, disgust. Sometimes the negotiator needs to be poker-faced, giving away nothing; but whilst following a strategy towards agreement, his expression should convey positive messages — cordiality, co-operation, vitality, pleasure.

Another aspect of influence is the use of silence. Consider the following dialogues:

Dialogue 'A'
'Surely you can reduce from £45,000 to £42,000?'
'Well, we really cannot do that because we are having great difficulty in meeting the deliveries that we have already promised and the costs of doing this would be pushed up by the overtime we would have to work, and there are problems of inflation anyway which cause us to be in great difficulty and we know from previous

experience what will happen if. . . . .'
Dialogue 'B'
'Surely you can reduce from £45,000 to £42,000?'
'No.'

Silence

A silence which must be broken by the questioner. A silence which is extremely forceful.

And finally, in these 'personal impact skills', we come to the visuals. They can be very powerful, and must be used with corresponding care.

The main dangers lie in putting forward too much visual material. It is all too easy to make the mistake of preparing a visual — a table or a graph — taking the trouble to make it look elegant, then finding that it simply damages the development of the negotiations. The human brain can absorb only a limited amount of information; it readily becomes dazzled and confused when presented with a complicated chart. If we should dazzle and confuse the Other Party, we damage the development of our negotiations.

Such an elegant chart also risks the N I H reaction — 'Not Invented Here'. It may be seen as a device brought in from the outside — something imposed on the group of two negotiating teams. And we do not like being imposed on.

The skilled negotiator therefore makes use of the powerful potential of visuals, but sparingly and carefully.

For example, the use of a simple statement or diagram on a flip-chart or blackboard has much to commend it, provided that the presenter takes the trouble, and more time than he might expect, to explain it fully to the Other Party. It is a device which is most helped when reinforcing an opening statement.

On the other hand, such a visual introduced in the middle of a negotiation is counter-productive. The Other Party's perception is that we have arrived at the negotiation with our minds made up about something; that we produce it half-way through the negotiation and therefore that our thinking has not been influenced by what they have said during the first half.

More positively influential is the visual drawn up during

the course of the meeting: the jotting or drawing or diagram created by one member of the group there and then, explaining as he goes along. It draws eyes, energy and concentration from anything else in the room towards the person of the presenter.

It does not matter how rough and ready it may be, it is something which we — the group of two teams — 'own' jointly. It is not something imposed from the outside. It is ours, we value it together, it is very influential.

Components of personal impact skills are therefore the ways in which the presenter uses his voice, his non-verbal skills, silences and visual aids. He should make use of these variables in presenting cases or statements prepared before the meeting; in the interventions which he makes; and in his pattern of attention while others are talking.

Summary

Negotiators see things from different viewpoints. This is natural, and unless they take positive steps they will be at the mercy of natural barriers to communication. They will fail to hear some points, distort others, and refuse to accept others again.

Practical steps to improve the communication between negotiators include:

1 Create a cordial and co-operative climate.
2 Make independent opening statements getting one another's position clarified independently. Do not seek to rebut before both pictures are clear.
3 Be aware of reasonable time frames. Don't talk too much or too long.
4 Prepare opening statements beforehand.
5 Present information simply, in digestible pieces.
6 Make good use of non-verbal communication — posture, gesture, eye-contact, visuals.
7 Listen well. Concentrate, take notes, seek to clarify, check with him that you've got it right.

7 Preparing for negotiations

It is critically important, when one's strategy is towards co-operation to mutual advantage, to build firm foundations at the start of the negotiation meeting. But before we can lay firm foundations, we must have made a good job of preparing the ground.

Time after time, one finds negotiators having two cries. On the one hand, 'We just didn't have time to do our preparation properly before the meeting'. On the other hand, after the meeting, 'Well, that has certainly taught me that I ought to be more careful about the way I prepare'.

There is no substitute for adequate preparation.

We shall deal with the subject in this chapter, making three sets of assumptions:

1 That the negotiator will have done his homework on the content issues for negotiation. That is, the buyer will have researched all specifications, quantities, market competition, market prices, etc. The banker will be aware of the availability of funds, the appropriate rate of interest, the status of the client, etc.

2 That the negotiator is familiar with the rules governing the negotiating territory. The company rules for pur-

chasing or for selling, the trade and/or international
rules that apply, the essential legal matters.
3 We assume that the deal is one which can be settled
within one or two meetings. (The more complex problem of extended negotiations is covered in chapter 17.)
This chapter will give suggestions about:

— conducting the preliminaries
— a general approach to the planning of negotiations
— the essence of the negotiating plan
— physical preparation.

Conducting the preliminaries

Other Party comes to a meeting bringing with him not only
knowledge of the basic facts. He brings also his own way of
conducting negotiations, his expectations about the way that
our Party will behave, and his counter-intentions.

Whether he has done his preparations sytematically or not
at all, he will bring impressions and opinions which will
influence his conduct.

To help him to bring the right attitudes and information,
we need to have explored beforehand as far as possible the
purpose of the meeting and the agenda of items which we
will discuss. This may have been done through correspondence
or by telephone or even, for major negotiations, through preliminary meetings between representatives.

A great deal of Other Party's basic values are deeply
engrained. We cannot much influence them during the preliminaries, but we can and do influence his opinions of us and
his expectations about the way we shall behave, which in turn
influence the way he will prepare to behave with us.

In part his expectations will be based on factors outside
our control, such as the stories he has heard about us, the sort
of relationship he would expect with a different Party in
our situation, and the experience he has had with other organisations in our own industry and culture.

He may have more direct evidence about us. Evidence from
dealings which he or his colleagues have had with our

organisation, evidence of the manner in which we negotiate and of the effectiveness with which we have implemented previous deals.

There remain however the preliminaries through which we can ourselves influence him. The manner in which we communicate beforehand needs to reflect our interest in dealing with him; our integrity; our co-operativeness. To create the most positive expectations we need to apply the basic ground rules for communication between people distant from one another: to be prompt and polite, clear, concise and correct.

We need also to be sensitive in the volume of our preliminary work. Sometimes we have to deal with businesses which seem virtually to resist paperwork. Such organisations always appreciate some brief statement on paper, covering issues like purpose, time and estimated duration; but with them, anything more than one sheet of paper is irritating and counter-productive.

For other organisations, where formality rules strongly, there is a need for meticulous detail in preliminary exchanges. Indeed, the preliminaries can escalate, almost to become the most important part of the negotiating process.

To summarise: it is important in the way we conduct the preliminaries to help the Other Party to prepare himself for the negotiations, and to ensure he enters the negotiating room looking forward to a desirable relationship.

General approach to planning

In principle, preparations for negotiation should lead to a plan which is simple and specific, yet flexible.

It must be sufficiently simple for the negotiator himself easily to carry the headlines in his own thinking. He must have these headlines, these principles of his plan, very clear in his mind; so clear, that he can handle the heavy on-going content of the negotiation with Other Party (making great demands on his conscious energy), yet at the same time subconsciously be able to relate to his plan.

Such simplicity is hard to achieve.

The plan must be specific: it cannot be simple without

being very specific. No room for reservations or elaborations.

Yet it must be flexible. The negotiator must be able to listen effectively to Other Party; to see the relationship of Other Party's thinking to his own plans; and to adjust flexibly.

So the aim of our preparation is to produce a plan which is simple and specific, yet flexible.

That is the ideal, but the reality is usually very different. The negotiator hunts out the information, reads through the correspondence in the files, talks to half a dozen colleagues with interest in the negotiation — each putting a different picture — and is under pressure to be on his way to the motorway or the airport with very little time to form this ragged mass of impulses into any coherent pattern.

His need now is for a discipline; for a general approach which he can use quickly and which he can apply to many different types of negotiation.

The general approach we use is in three stages:

> Ideas stage
> Thesis sentence
> Analysis stage.

The aim of the *ideas stage* is to make a quick review of the area for negotiation and at the same time to clear one's own mind. It corresponds to the brain-storming stage in 'Preparation of information', but is now in two steps. Step one is quickly to jot down all one's jumbled ideas about the negotiation. This would be as shown in Figure 6.9. Step two is to jot down our thoughts about Other Party on another sheet of paper. What they do, where they are, what they look like, what we know of the individuals, what we know they want from the negotiation, what we guess they want, and what else we would like to know. Again, random thoughts (Figure 7.1).

This ideas stage has led us to the production of two sheets of paper. One with random ideas on the subject and one with random ideas on the Other Party. Having been filled in, having got our minds cleared, these sheets have already largely served their purpose. They should now be put away (not necessarily thrown away — they just might serve some useful purpose later in our preparations).

Our conscious energy is now free to prepare our plans,

<u>Jensen Electric Supply</u>

30 years relationship   Know our

Annual golf match   processes

Good customers   Keep it friendly

Tough but fair

Enjoy dealing

Probably see Alf

Hope not Doug

Are they in trouble?

Maybe need help

Maybe we need to
       protect

Is whole region in
       trouble

Or just them?

Fig. 7.1 Random thoughts about Other Party

uncluttered by the jumble of thoughts that was previously there; and the first step in this *analytical stage* is to prepare a thesis sentence.

This thesis sentence is a statement in general terms of what we hope to achieve from the negotiation process. It is a statement for our own guidance, and may sometimes differ from the general purpose of the negotiation as defined to/ agreed with Other Party.

The thesis sentence needs to be simple, so we should try to specify it within a maximum of fifteen to twenty words. If it takes more, the negotiator has not sufficiently simplified his thinking about why he is entering the negotiating process.

It is critical that his thinking should be so sharp. If he finds it difficult to state his purpose within twenty words, then he needs to spend more time on clearing his mind, drafting his thoughts about the purpose of the meeting, then pruning and modifying until he gets inside the maximum of twenty words (Figure 7.2).

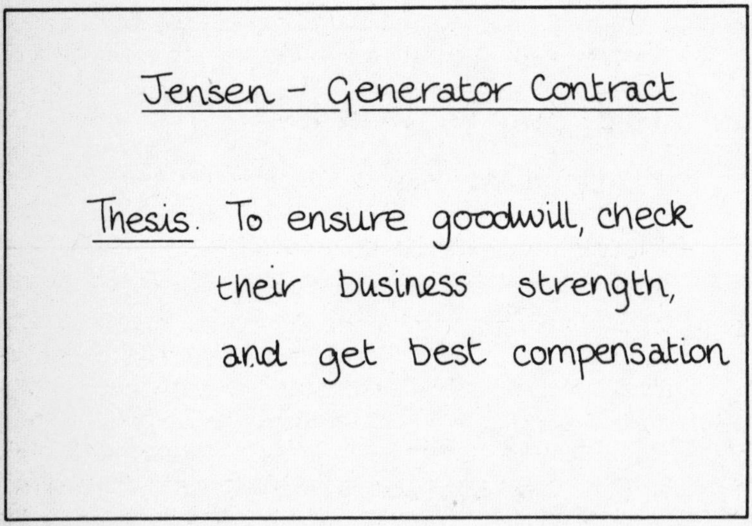

Fig. 7.2 Thesis sentence

Continuing the analysis stage the second step is to develop a plan for handling the negotiation meeting.

The need now is to produce an ordered approach to the conduct of the negotiation, together with a statement of one's opening position.

The essence of the plan

The control of any meeting hinges on three of the 'Four P's' which we identified in chapter 2: the Purpose of the meeting, the Plan for the meeting and the Pace of the meeting. (The Personalities element, the introduction of the people and their roles, should be a routine, not a part of the plan specific to any one meeting.) Our preparation must cover those 3 P's.

> The *Purpose* spelt out in one sentence which can be offered to Other Party as 'our view of the purpose of this meeting'. It should be 'our declared view' of the purpose, not necessarily the same as the thesis sentence. The *Plan* or agenda must be kept simple. The human brain has the ability to keep a clear image of only a few agenda topics throughout a negotiation meeting. About four main items. If in the preparation one tries to give equal significance to say seven or eight main points — then the brain is over-stretched. It cannot later have a sharp recollection of so many main points. It cannot easily, during the negotiation, relate all that is going on to the prepared plan.
> So at the analysis stage we are concerned to prepare our plans for the negotiation meeting under about four main headings.
> The *Pace* — in terms of 'how long' — should also be estimated.

The practical way to go about this preparation is — after going through the brain-storming stage and preparing the thesis sentence — to plan the agenda. Aim for the ideal of *four* main agenda points, sub-heading each if need be.

> In negotiations 'Towards Agreement', a sequence I regularly find useful is — 'Ours — Theirs — Creative possibilities — Practical actions'. 'Ours' may, in one session, be 'what we hope for from the negotiation',

with the corresponding 'theirs' being what they hope for; then the creative possibilities for the two of us working together; and finally – what we should do before we meet again.

In a later session, the same sequence might become – 'our offer – their offer – overlaps and problems – action needed to resolve problems'.

And for the next meeting – 'Where we'd got to and what we each had to do – our new position – their new position – what is agreed and what remains to be done'.

Having got the plan worked out, we should 'top' it with a statement of Purpose (already considered when building our Thesis Sentence, though not necessarily to be repeated verbatim); and we should 'tail' it with an estimate of the time we shall need (Figure 7.3).

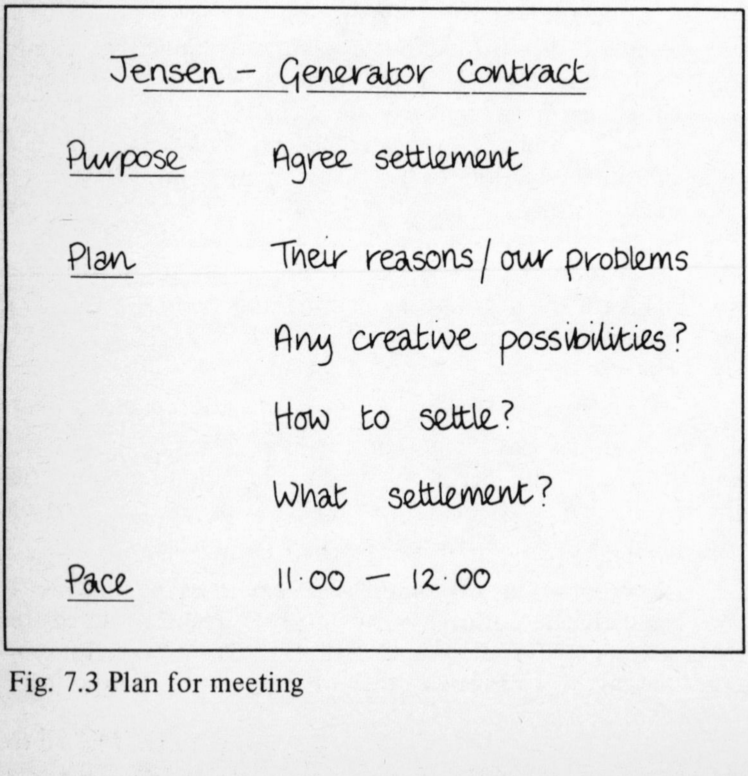

```
Jensen – Generator Contract

Purpose     Agree settlement

Plan        Their reasons / our problems

            Any creative possibilities?

            How to settle?

            What settlement?

Pace        11·00 – 12·00
```

Fig. 7.3 Plan for meeting

Finally, the plan needs reducing to key words printed on a postcard.

The purpose of this final stage of planning is to provide a document which the negotiator can have in front of him in the negotiating room. He then needs the key statements prominent and visible at one glance of the eyes. He needs them as prompters for his sub-conscious, so that he can still control the negotiating process, even when his conscious energy is absorbed in the content of the negotiation (Figure 7.4).

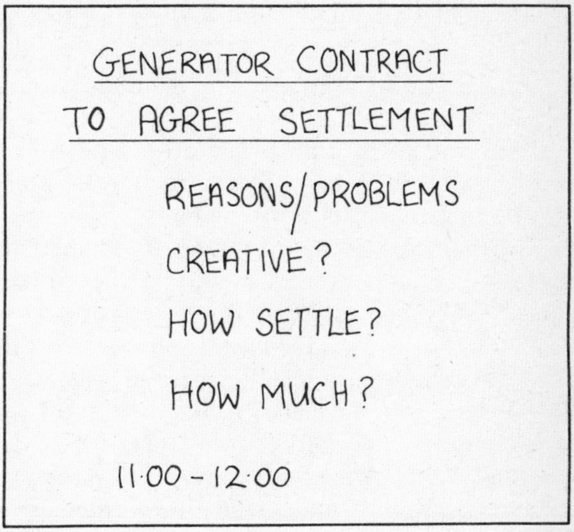

Fig. 7.4 Prompter for control of negotiation

In addition to this procedural preparation for a negotiation, there is another item to which we have already attached much importance. This is the Opening Statement to be made at the outset of the negotiating process. It should be systematically prepared, using the methods set out in chapter 6 on 'Presenting Information'.

Following this preliminary work the negotiator goes into the negotiating room properly prepared both to control the process of negotiating, and to present his own position.

What about the room he is going into?

The physical preparation

In this section we shall look briefly at the negotiating room, the layout of the room and the need for services.

The negotiating room itself needs to have the obvious facilities — light, heating, air, noise-proofing.

More contentious are the furnishing and the layout of the room. Negotiators seem to need a table at which to be seated — they seem to feel defenceless without a table between them. But what sort of table? A rectangular table — or the typical businessman's desk — leads to parties being seated opposite to one another. This immediately creates a head-on physical confrontation.

Negotiators recognise that they feel differently on the rare occasions when they sit at round tables. In any poll of negotiators there will be a hefty majority who find it more comfortable and more constructive to use a round table than to use either a rectangular or a square one.

Should negotiators, whether at round or rectangular tables, split into their respective teams or should they intermix? It depends on the mood and style of the negotiations.

Where the parties are relaxed and collaborative, then the relaxation and collaboration is heightened by intermixing. At the extreme this would lead to each negotiator in a team being seated between two negotiators from the Other Party; but that would be contrived only by a formal approach to seating positions. Within an agreement-oriented group, the ice-breaking period leads to informality in the choice of seating positions. It is a purely random matter as to whether one walks up to the table with and sits beside a member of Own or of Other Party.

Where the negotiation process is more conflicting, then it is natural that the parties will gather together, probably on opposite sides of the table. This is both for psychological and for practical reasons. Psychologically, the mood is of 'all together against them'. Practically, either Party may want to refer to papers which they want to keep obscured from Others (impracticable if Others are neighbours) or they may want to sit together so that they can pass notes within their team.

Incidentally neither the regular reference to secret papers nor the passing of notes are symbols of good negotiators. Energy is needed for the exchanges with Other Party and not for private transactions. It is more skilful to take a recess, either to check on the private papers, or to handle private communication with colleagues.

It is not only the shape of table that is important — it is also size. There is a comfortable distance at which individuals or groups of individuals may sit from one another. If the parties are sitting a little closer, then the atmosphere becomes warmer. If they are sitting a lot closer then they become uncomfortable and heated. If the distance apart is, on the other hand, too much, then the parties become remote and the discussion becomes academic.

Apart from the question of the room and the furnishing, the host needs to make suitable provisions for sustenance and for the well being of Other Party. A special courtesy is in providing Other Party with a room which they can use for recesses, together with such other facilities as typing, telex and telephone.

Summary

1 The preparation for a negotiation meeting needs discipline. It needs time and the regular use of the same approach.

2 We suggest a disciplined approach of:

   (a) brain-storming
   (b) thesis sentence
   (c) planning

3 The preparation needs to cover purpose, plan and pace of the meeting.

4 The Opening Statement should be prepared equally carefully.

5 Physical arrangements influence the form of the subsequent negotiations.

Finale to Part I

The aim in Part 1 of this book has been to review some of the
abilities of skilled negotiators. Specifically, to review those
skills which enable two parties to negotiate 'Towards Agreement' to their joint advantage.

Key elements in this pattern of negotiations are:

1 To create a climate which is cordial and co-operative,
   brisk and businesslike.
2 To start by agreeing on a procedure which will lead the
   parties to work to the same agreed end, along agreed
   lines, at an agreed speed.
3 To progress along a broad front avoiding the in-fighting
   of vertical negotiations.
4 To explore the possibilities, starting from independent
   Opening Statements, moving into creative and
   imaginative development of joint ideas; but checking
   that this open strategy remains sensible before getting
   too deeply committed.
5 To make occasional use of agreement oriented tactics.
6 To sustain the spirit and process of the negotiation,
   summarising progress, recapitulating agreement, and
   keeping to agreed plan.

7 To communicate skilfully — create the right conditions, keep it simple, listen diligently, use 'personal impact' skills.

8 To have prepared systematically before entering the negotiating room.

These are basic skills. Many negotiators might want to check their effectiveness in these skills: we have therefore provided a check-list for them on the facing page.

We suggest that the reader uses that check-list as follows:

1 Take two or three photocopies.

2 Fill in one copy, drawing up a profile of your own skills — what you're very good at, what you're not at all good at, and what lies in between.

3 With a different coloured pen, put in another profile, on the same copy: a *realistic* ambition of the skill level to which you might develop.

4 Get a couple of knowledgeable colleagues to draw up on the other copies, and to discuss with you their views of your actual and potential skills.

5 Decide what skills you need to develop.

6 For each skill which you wish to develop, set down on a separate sheet the specific steps you could take to improve your performance. If in doubt, read again the relevant chapter or section in Part 1.

7 Make a diary note for three months ahead, to check your new effectiveness against the targets you set yourself at step 5.

Check-list for skills 'Towards Agreement'

	Preparation	Climate formation	Planning and control of agenda	Exploration	Presentation of views	Listening skills	Using creative tactics	Personal impact
10								
9								
8								
7								
6								
5								
4								
3								
2								
1								

Part II

To our advantage

Prologue

In this second part of the book, we shall be concerned with a different pattern of negotiation.

We now look at the skills needed to gain an advantage for our own party. This will, of course, involve some of the skills we discussed for working 'Towards Agreement'; but we shall be approaching the negotiation with a different attitude, using some skills differently, and introducing a range of further skills.

Negotiating 'to our advantage' needs different attitudes and a different approach (chapter 8).

The bidding and bargaining phases become relatively more important (chapters 9 to 10) and tactics 'to our advantage' are either different, or are used differently (chapter 11).

Negotiating 'to our advantage' is different from setting out to 'win battles' to which we devote chapter 12.

In the second part of the book, the experienced negotiator will find a number of ideas to help him in polishing his skills. For the less experienced negotiator, this will be new territory.

8 The approach 'to our advantage'

There are often good reasons for the negotiator to concentrate on getting the best deal for his own party. He may be negotiating in a situation where this approach will produce the most satisfactory results. Or he may be negotiating with Others whose behaviour presses him to operate in this way.

To help him in developing the approach, this chapter will look at:

1 The attitudes demanded by this strategy.
2 The basic method.
3 Opening to our advantage.
4 Conduct to our advantage.

Attitudes

Our objective is now to negotiate to our advantage.

This does not necessarily mean 'to his disadvantage'. This distinction — 'not to his disadvantage' — is so important that we start with a little story to illustrate.

Jack Jones wanted to buy a ring for his girlfriend. He had saved about £400 and was going on saving at £20 a week.

When he went to Smith's Jewellers shop, his eye was caught by a ring priced at £750. He felt that this was just the thing for his girlfriend but, of course, could not afford it. Smith's were very sorry — indeed they said that he might be able to get it in the sales in a couple of weeks time, but more probably it would have been sold in the meantime.

Sadly, he went round to Brown's. They had a trayful of rings which were quite similar but cost only £500. He felt he might have to settle for one of these, but decided he would first return to Smith's in a couple of weeks in the hope that the £750 ring was not yet sold.

Fortunately it was not. The ring was reduced by 20 per cent — a saving of £150, so that it was on offer at £600. He was very enthusiastic but still had not enough money to buy. He talked to the manager who — anxious to help — offered a 10 per cent special discount for cash. Jack gave him £450 on the nail, promised to come back with the £90 by the end of the month, and walked away delighted.

So was his girlfriend. She was thrilled to have this £750 ring. Jack had all the satisfaction of having saved and striven for it and secured it despite the chance that it could have been sold to someone else. They were both very happy indeed.

So, of course, were Smith's. Like Brown's, they had bought rings from the wholesalers for £300. They had shown a profit of £240 — even though Brown's had all along been offering the same goods for £500. But the same goods from Brown's had not attracted Jack Jones. He got satisfaction from Smith's, not from Brown's.

Was it a fair deal? This depends on what we mean by a fair deal. If the above story had not included the information that Brown's were selling the same ring cheaper, we would obviously have thought, both parties being satisfied, that it was a fair deal. And this is the condition under which most negotiations take place: we do not normally have an objective standard (like Brown's price) against which we can judge success or failure.

In my view the criterion of a 'fair deal' is that it should be equally satisfactory to both parties.

Or equally unsatisfactory.

The basic method

Other Party's satisfaction is not absolute, but depends on the way he values things. The underlying attitude then of negotiating 'to our advantage' has to be that this is not to Other's disadvantage: it is rather to find the best way (in our interests) of giving them the most possible satisfaction.

The skilled negotiator working to own advantage is therefore constantly trying to influence the way Other Party values things.

In the Jack Jones example, Jack valued the fact that he was getting a £750 ring. He valued the fact that it was a unique ring, one which might be sold before the sale. He was glad of his wisdom in waiting a couple of weeks for the sales reduction. He was delighted that his discussion with the manager got him a further 10 per cent.

Each step in Smith's negotiating strategy was designed to give just that sense of satisfaction:

- the price the goods had been valued at
- the sense of uniqueness of the ring
- the sense of achievement he got from negotiating
- the sense of achievement in settling the deal.

all combined to give him satisfaction — and to build advantage for the sellers.

The underlying method used by the negotiator 'to our advantage' is one of ensuring that Others are satisfied whilst we achieve what we want.

One final illustration of the attitude: we are no longer trying to make the biggest possible cake. We are now trying to share the cake to our best satisfaction. It will not be fair if either party gets more than half the cake. But maybe it is to our preference to get more of the fruit in the cake, especially if we can help him to relish more of the icing. So both parties will feel they end up with the tastier part. Both parties will get 60 percent of the satisfaction which the cake could give.

Opening to our advantage

In this style of negotiating, we shall each be concerned to identify how we can give satisfaction to the Other while still securing the advantage we ourselves want.

We must therefore be very clear about the advantage that we want. We must approach the negotiation with a firm set of objectives. Clear, precise, and wherever possible, in figures. Our preparation needs to be very systematic, and to lead us to more precise aims and targets than we sought when looking for creative negotiation.

Within the negotiating process, we are constantly concerned to find out where his interests lie and where we can give him satisfaction most readily.

Some very experienced negotiators accordingly enter a negotiation with great concern to understand what Others will value. They enter with some knowledge of the qualities which Others esteem − be they technical, or packaging, or pricing, or delivery, or integrity, or . . . . They are anxious to get further information quickly. 'How's business?', they ask; because if Other Party is short of business then he can be satisfied quite differently from when he is overloaded with work.

'How are you finding cash flow?' − because this will influence satisfaction from the sort of terms we can agree.

'What is your experience of deliveries?' − because again this will influence the satisfaction element in negotiating deliveries.

Some experienced negotiators make great use of such openings. I am not convinced that they are wise. Other Party's reaction to such questions is always likely to be guarded to avoid giving away critical information. In any case, my impression is that negotiators are generally poor at recognising what Other really wants: they see the whole pattern of negotiation so much from their own standpoint that if they try too early to guess Other's position, they impose their own values on to it.

Moreover such early probing puts Other Party on the defensive and prompts them straight away to start countering our thrusts. We're on the way to a fight.

How then should we conduct the opening moves in developing the negotiation to our advantage?

The opening phase of 'creating the climate' remains important; but not as important as before. We still need some period of ice-breaking, so that we can come to communicate with Other Party and deal with them on the same wavelength. But we no longer need to establish such a cordial and collaborative atmosphere. Pleasant, brisk and businesslike will do.

We are still wise to seek for an agreed plan: one which we can use to control the discussion in a businesslike manner. But we are no longer so concerned to keep the emphasis on agreement. Now we may see positive advantages to our side in getting some particular sequence on the agenda: and we would prefer to start the ball rolling on that issue rather than spend a lot of time underlining 'process' agreement.

This means that in opening a negotiation to our advantage we are going to put less energy than previously into the stages of climate formation and into the opening process. We are going to get into the content of the negotiation as quickly as possible.

Conduct to our advantage

Negotiating in this style, starting with a firm and precise view of our objectives, we shall also tend to short-cut the exploratory phase. We shall, of course, need to take steps to shape up a prospective deal: — but our interests are less in working creatively with Other to shape a deal, more in getting the best advantage to ourselves from the sort of deal we expect.

We soon come to the phase of issue selection. And this becomes the first main area in which we will seek to develop fresh skills.

This choice and sequence of the issues on which the parties will work, often becomes itself a preliminary round of negotiation. If They are believed to want to put priority on price, and we want to put priority on delivery — then it is to our advantage to have the delivery issue on the agenda ahead of price. It would give us a chance to see how far They are prepared to make concessions to us, before we came under pressure to make concessions on delivery. We would then be better equipped to decide on our concession pattern: we would know better how much and how quickly it would be prudent for us to give way.

Such putting of priority to agenda items is seen by many people as the critical opening skirmish in negotiations.

People who write on this matter have a sequence they favour for issue selection, and they are unanimous in their views:

1 First work on an issue not too important to us, on which we can afford to make a concession and to show our readiness to compromise.
2 Then another issue not too important, on which we can test their pattern of negotiation and concessions.
3 An issue of critical importance to us (but of course not revealed as so important) on which we shall look for serious concessions from them.
4 Then other major issues, followed by minor issues.
5 Reserve till the end, one minor issue on which we can afford to give ground as a final gesture toward settling.

Note that this sequence assumes that the pattern of negotiating will be vertical (discussion of each issue separately). I respect that weight of opinion; but I still believe that more is achieved by negotiating laterally (small moves on a broad front), and I use my energy on trying to create that lateral process. It is only under strong pressure from an intransigent Other Party that I get into skirmishes on issue selection.

The phases of exploration, bidding, bargaining and settling must, of course, be followed through; but the pattern may become one of going through each phase on a first issue (e.g. price), then each phase on a second issue (e.g. delivery), etc. – the 'vertical' pattern.

Communication retains critical importance. Indeed, when negotiating to separate advantage, there is an increased chance that the parties will come into conflict, increasing the problems of communication between them and needing even more skill in the process we discussed at length in chapter 6.

In the process of conducting the negotiations, we are going to be concerned to get our advantage whilst giving the Other Party satisfaction. The Other Party will not be satisfied simply by our offering an easy solution, any more than Jack Jones was attracted by Brown's £500 price. Nor will they be satisfied by our compromising too readily. We must therefore be prepared to take up an extreme position and to go on defending it for a long while — knowing full well that Other Party too (in this style of negotiation) will be taking up and defending extreme positions.

Our conduct therefore will need to bring in elements of bluffing and even of brinkmanship, which we did not even consider when our interests were 'Towards Agreement'.

We will need to apply this conduct in the phases of bidding and bargaining on which we are about to embark.

Summary

1 Negotiating to our advantage does not necessarily mean 'to Other's disadvantage'.
2 We must aim to give him satisfaction from the deal whilst keeping a keen eye on our advantage.
3 We must therefore start with a precise definition for ourselves of 'our advantage'.
4 We need to create a brisk and businesslike climate and to have a plan for the meeting — preferably an agreed plan.
5 We shall move quickly into the content of the negotiation.
6 The process of selecting issues and putting them in sequence for discussion becomes an important element of the negotiation, but still a 'broad front' approach is recommended.
7 The process of negotiation will involve degrees of bluffing and counter-bluffing.

9 Bidding

The plan for this chapter is to break the subject of bidding into four main sections:

1 Generalisations.
2 Choice of opening bid.
3 Presentation of bid.
4 Responsiveness.

Generalisations

The pattern of bidding and bargaining is seen by many people to be the kernel of the negotiating process.

Where that view is held, then the manner in which people act leads bidding and bargaining to be indeed the kernel of the process; and even when negotiators are more interested in creativity, the skills of bidding and bargaining remain highly important. They have the potential on the one hand to win or lose a project; on the other, to win at a profit — or at a loss.

In my experience the majority of bids in negotiations are determined by commercial people. People reared in a commercial tradition of dealing with other people of kindred spirit. Commercial people with a wealth of experience and an intuitive sense of the on-going market possibilities.

I would not claim the competence to criticise the bids which such people make. I do know that when I myself make such bids, based on my commercial beliefs about a market, I have often been proved wrong. I have sold goods and services for two-thirds the price for which other negotiators subsequently sold the same goods and services. I have tried to buy goods 10 per cent or 20 per cent cheaper than offered, and have failed to make the purchase at all.

I am not appalled at such mistakes. Given all the evidence that I had at the time and given the circumstances at that time, I think that the bids were as reasonable as I could then have made them. But I have certainly learned from these experiences, both in terms of my approaches to buying and in terms of my approaches to selling. In particular, I have learned to set my sights high, whether buying or selling.

It remains my overriding belief that the best guide to bidding decisions is the commercial judgement of experienced commercial people.

There are of course other approaches, including a wealth of theory about bidding. This is to be found principally in the writings of economists and econometrists. The essence of this theoretical writing is that a bid should be made at the point which gives the best combination of (a) utility to the bidder and (b) success probability. Intellectually, this is elegant and satisfying; but for practical purposes, it is not found to be of much help by most negotiators.

There are of course some circumstances under which such high cost approaches are entirely justified. For example, in the oil industry in bidding for Exploration Plots, where tens or hundreds of millions of dollars are at stake, teams of mathematicians work with computers using such theories, to advise on bids (reference 8). But within this book, we are concerned with practical skills, and we need more down to earth guides to bidding.

The choice of bid

Negotiating to our advantage, the guideline is to start with the *highest defensible bid*. (For buyers, the corresponding phrase is of course 'lowest defensible offer'.)

The opening bid needs to be 'the highest' because:

1 The opening bid sets a limit beyond which we cannot aspire. Having once made it, we cannot normally put in a higher bid at a later stage — at any rate not with hope of the higher bid being accepted.
2 Our first bid influences Others in their valuation of our offer.
3 A high bid gives scope for manoeuvre during the later bargaining phases. It gives us something in reserve with which to trade.
4 The opening bid has a real influence on the final settlement level. The higher we aspire the more we shall achieve.

In seminars with experienced negotiators, people who are used to working internationally and handling major deals, I regularly use a simple case study which dramatically shows the need to bid high. Realistically it is possible to settle the case anywhere within the range of £100,000 to £850,000.

> I have had both results. In one case, Team A negotiated a settlement with Team B at £850,000. On another occasion, using exactly the same case material but with different team members, a different Team A settled for £100,000.
>
> Of course, there is an average around which the results cluster when used by different negotiators. About £300,000 is an average, but 30 per cent of results fall outside the range £200,000 to £400,000.
>
> Why?

There are many reasons, but one of the factors is always aspiration. If Team A starts by bidding £300,000, then it will not end up with a better than average result. If Team B starts by offering £300,000, then it, too, will fail to beat par.

Such staggering differences between the ambition of different negotiators with the same brief can only be explained by differences in their level of aspiration. The optimistic negotiator, the one who starts the bidding at £1,000,000 is astonished later to learn that other people were prepared to start as low as (say) £400,000. The pessimistic negotiator, the one who started at £300,000, is equally astonished to hear that anybody might have started as high as £1,000,000.

The opening bid needs to be high. At the same time it must be defensible. Putting forward a bid which cannot be defended does positive damage to the negotiating process. It is found to be offensive by the Other Party; and if we cannot defend that bid when challenged in subsequent bargaining, we lose face, we lose credibility, we are fast forced into retreat.

The content of the bid of course usually needs to cover a range of issues. The components of the opening bid in a commercial negotiation will not simply be price, but a combination of price, delivery, payment terms, quality specification and a dozen other items.

The 'highest defensible bid' is not an absolute figure, it is a figure which is relevant to the particular circumstances. It is, specifically, a figure which relates to the way in which Others are operating. If they are pressing to their advantage, then for our advantage we must press with a very high bid. If we face a lot of competition, then we must tailor our opening bid to the level at which it at least enables us to be invited to continue the negotiations. If we have established cordial relationships with Others, possibly over a long period of time, then we shall know the style in which they will operate and the degree of co-operation we can expect — we know the level at which it is prudent for us to make our bid.

On each individual item the opening bid needs to be the highest defensible. We are certain, when negotiating to our advantage, to be pushed by Others to compromise on one or two issues; we cannot be sure which until the bargaining process is under way; we must aspire high on all issues and keep room to manoeuvre.

Presentation of bid

The opening bid needs to be put firmly. Without reservations.
Without hesitations. So that it may carry the conviction of
a conscientious negotiating party.

It needs to be put clearly so that the Other Party recognises precisely what we are asking. The creation of a visual,
i.e. taking a sheet of paper and writing figures on it, within
the sight of the Other Party, whilst one is stating the bid —
this is powerful reinforcement to the clarity of the bid.

It should be put without apology or comment. There is no
need to apologise for anything that can be defended. There
is no need to comment since the Other Party can be expected
to raise questions on matters which concern it. And
voluntary comment (before Other make the request) simply
makes them aware that we are concerned about issues which
they might never have considered.

Those then are three guidelines to the way in which a bid
should be presented: firmly, clearly, without comment.

There may — at any rate in collaborative negotiations —
be a need to precede the bidding with statements showing
our approach to the subject.

> Taking again the 'cancelled contract' case (chapter 6),
> the seller should, before the bidding, have offered his
> views about the legal situation. Within English law he
> should have put the point: 'My understanding of the
> legal position is that we are entitled to the full value of
> the contract. From this can be deducted any costs we
> have saved, and the value of any replacement orders we
> are able to book. In addition, we are entitled to disloc-
> ation expenses. Considering all these items I think the
> lawyers would probably come up with a figure of
> £X00,000.'

The negotiator — assuming a collaborative approach —
should have made this statement during the exploratory
phase whilst still trying with the Other Party to establish
their respective perspectives.

The competitive bidder, for whom there is likely to be
much less of an exploratory approach, needs to put his bid

more forcefully. 'Well, now let's get down to business and to settling this matter. We have considered the matter carefully and taken advice, and we are entitled to compensation of £800,000.' Full Stop.

There is some controversy as to who should be the first to make a bid. Is it an advantage or a disadvantage to bid ahead of Other? The advantages are associated with the establishment of influence. The Party who makes the first bid is the first to establish one of the brackets within which settlement will ultimately take place. And this first statement in the bidding carries a durable influence throughout the subsequent negotiating/bargaining. First bid is more influential than responsive bid.

A disadvantage is that when Other Party hears our opening bid, they can make some final adjustment in their own thinking. They have this new element of information about our starting point, and can modify their own bidding to gain fresh advantage.

> Given the fact that we are asking for £800,000, they might open the bidding at £100,000. But before they had heard our opening bid they might have been quite prepared to open at £150,000 or even more.

Another disadvantage is that Others may try to force on us a 'follow-my-leader' pattern of bargaining. That is, they may try to concentrate on attacking our bid, trying to drive us down and down without giving us any information about their own position. This is something we must resist – we must make them bid and not allow the negotiation to degenerate into a fight on our first offer.

So which pattern do we want to follow? On balance is it to our advantage that we should open the bidding or that they should? On balance, it is usually to our advantage to make the influential first bid if we can anticipate that the negotiation is going to be competitive in character; and if we have followed a disciplined procedure, we shall be well aware of the character which negotiations will take before we get to the bidding stage.

The issue of 'who should open' is less clear in more collaborative conditions. Indeed where those conditions are

strong, the parties often sense their way into a probable
settlement without having to go through any very difficult
phase of bidding and bargaining. Their explorations enable
them together to recognise the reasonable settlement position.

Responsiveness

In responding to bids by the Other Party there is a need to
distinguish between clarification and justification.

The competent negotiator first ensures that he knows
what the Other Party is bidding. Precisely. He asks any
questions which are needed to ensure than he gets the
picture correct. He makes sure, in the process, that the Other
Party recognises that these are questions for clarification,
and not demands to justify. And once satisfied, he sum-
marises his understanding of the Other Party's bid, as a check
on the effectiveness of communication between them.

First Party should at this stage deflect questions which
demand that he justifies his position. He has put a bid, and
he has a perfect right to know what Other is prepared to
offer in return.

> Others may well ask their question clarifying *what* his
> bid is, but they should not be allowed to go into *why*
> he makes that bid, or *how* he has calculated it, until
> they have given their bid in return.

Summary

And so we reach the stage of negotiations at which the
Parties have made their opening bids.

1 Those bids should be the highest defensible.
2 They should be put firmly, clearly, without apology or
  hesitation.
3 The level of the bid depends on the extent to which the
  negotiation is competitive or collaborative.
4 Each side should have taken steps to ensure that it has
  got clear the bid being made by the Other Party.
5 Each should deflect demands for justification until it

has got Other's position clear.

From this understanding of the opening bids, collaborative parties should be able (after all their joint exploration and creativity) quickly to perceive the prospects for settlement and to move rapidly in that direction. Competitive negotiators on the other hand will be moving into a new and important phase of bargaining.

10 Bargaining

Satisfaction is not absolute. Satisfaction depends on the way people value things.

Negotiating to our advantage, we must conduct the bargaining phase to our advantage so that Other Party gets satisfaction. We need to let him have some extra icing which we care little for, provided that we can secure the majority of the fruit for ourselves.

In this process, we must be careful not to give him too much icing too quickly. Both because he relishes several small helpings more than one big one; and because he is likely to part only slowly with portions of the fruit.

Bargaining to our advantage, we are concerned to make a fair deal in which both parties will be equally satisfied.

Or equally dissatisfied. If it is not possible for us to cut the cake so that we both get what we want (icing and fruit respectively) − then we must bargain in such a way that the dissatisfaction will be equally shared between us.

To give a framework for these skills of bargaining, this chapter will consider:

1 The moves we must make at the outset.
2 The way to influence the deal.
3 Making concessions.

4 Breaking an impasse.
5 Towards a settlement.

At the outset

As we start the bargaining process, we need to take two steps:

1 Get it clear.
2 Assess the situation.

It is vital to establish a clear picture of Other Party's requirements at the outset. We must have a clear picture of *what* he is bidding already — at least we should have done so in the bidding phase. But at that time, our main concern was to get a clear picture of what his bid was, without yet being worried as to *why* he should be making such a bid.

Now we need to know why. We need increasingly to build an understanding of what will give him satisfaction and of how we can trade to our advantage whilst continuing to give him satisfaction.

We must discover what for him are essentials and what else is desirable but not essential. We must find out what aspects of his bid are really of fringe interest only — where he could readily give.

To achieve this clarity, the guidelines for our behaviour have to be:

1 Check every item of his bid. Enquire why. Ask how important the item is and how much flexibility he could introduce.
2 Never speculate on his opinions or on his motives. Never put words into his mouth.
  A speculation only irritates. Moreover it is often misconceived — it is out of our frame of reference, not his, and confuses the negotiation between us.
3 Note his answers without comment. Reserve our position. Avoid deep diving or premature diving into any issue. Keep it on a broad front.

Correspondingly, in the stage of the bargaining process

when he is getting our position clear, we should limit our answers to the minimum. Give him the essentials which he asks for and do not go into extensive comments or justifications.

Having now 'got our thoughts straight' we come to the stage at which we need to assess the situation. We should:

- assess the differences between us
- analyse Other Party's real position
- take a first decision
- prepare for the next round.

There will be *differences* between the parties. The differences can be of three categories — imaginary, invented or real.

Imaginary differences are those which arise when the parties do not properly understand what one another require; or alternatively do not accept that the Other Party's statement properly reflects its requirement. These imaginary differences arise from defective communication and the cure is to develop more skill in communicating.

Invented differences are those where one party is creating a bluff. Specifying some stance or bid simply to give further manoeuvring room for further steps of negotiation. The cure for invented differences lies in putting aside more time for negotiating, going on to successive rounds, modifying one's own bids whilst whittling down the Other Party's inventions. It is a time consuming game of bluff and counter-bluff.

Real differences need other treatment. They need the skills we will be considering shortly in the section on 'influencing the deal'.

Having assessed the differences between us as far as possible, we need to *analyse* Other Party's real position. We must be cautious here because we cannot know for certain what they really want. We can take all they have said, we can check not only what they have said but the way in which they said it, and we can also think of their situation and of their normal patterns of behaviour. But with all this information, we shall

never be certain that we are right: we shall always, to some
extent, be guessing.

This is why it has been so important at the outset to probe
their reasoning and their priorities.

Our analysis needs to distinguish:

1 What they will accept.
2 What they will not accept.
3 The strength of their requirements on each issue.
4 The probable settlement area.

This 'probable settlement area' is in fact recognised by
experienced negotiators at the end of the first round of
bidding. Having established and evaluated the opening
bids they can make a pretty good guesstimate of the likely
final settlement between the parties. Indeed they proceed in
ways which lead them now − not necessarily quickly −
towards the predicted position.

Assuming significant differences between the parties, we
now have three options open to us:

1 We can accept.
2 We can reject.
3 We can carry on negotiating.

If we decide to carry on negotiating, then we must *prepare
for the next round*. Our options at this stage are:

1 A new offer from us (orally, or in writing).
2 Seek a new offer from them (orally, or in writing).
3 Change the shape of the deal (vary the quantity, or the
   quality, or the use of third parties, or the timing or the
   financing, or . . . .).
   Find some change of shape which will give us better
   scope for agreement.
4 Embark on give-and-take bargaining.

The steps in preparing for that give-and-take are:

− issue identification. Make a list of all the issues which
we can see in the package to be negotiated.
− assess their style. Since we have come so far in the
process of negotiating with them, it is likely that both

parties are negotiating 'to own advantage'.

But even with this similarity of style, there can be differences of degree. One organisation with whom we negotiate may habitually prolong the negotiations, taking every step to gain advantage; another may look for short cuts and be ready to move much more quickly. And it is always possible that the Other Party may be aggressive fighters, for whom we will need to use yet another group of tactics.

— analyse the issues. Decide which of them are essential for us and which are points on which we could concede a little.

— then prepare our bargaining position:

(a) An essential conditions list. Those issues on which we cannot respectably concede anything.

(b) A concessions list. Those issues on which we could possibly concede, with against each a progression stepped from minimum to maximum (Figure 10.1).

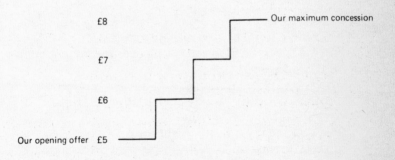

Fig. 10.1 Concession list for price

— open each negotiation meeting with a new round of climate formation and of agreeing the procedure
— end each round by establishing means to resolve outstanding difficulties.

At the outset of the bargaining phase then we need to establish what the Other Party really wants, then to assess the situation; to assess the differences between us, to analyse the strengths of their respective arguments and to prepare for the next round. Our preparation needs to be particularly extended if we are going to enter a pattern of give-and-take.

Influencing the deal

There are two ways in which we can influence the deal. One is to influence the negotiator; the other is to influence the situation.

To make the point about influencing the negotiator let me tell you about two different negotiators who seem to have quite different abilities to influence other people.

> David Crewe is a bright, young negotiator.
>
> Ernest Hargreaves has been around for a long time. David is very clever and is always awake for the last ounce of negotiating possibility.
>
> Ernest is relatively dull. He does not seem to worry too much about the pennies.
>
> David is quick to see a point, prompt in his replies and quickly able to take in everything that is said.
>
> Ernest is slower. He keeps going over the same ground time and again.
>
> David is completely rational.
>
> Ernest is slightly woolly and irrational. Other Party often has to put him right.
>
> David continually puts up bright ideas.
>
> Ernest seems to be a little bit slow in thinking of creative possibilities. In fact often I have to suggest things which maybe be could have seen.
>
> David is to the point, recognising the differences between us and not being reluctant to get them into the open. He tells me, 'You are being aggressive'.
>
> Ernest does not seem to see the point so quickly. His corresponding statement is, 'It seems to me that I could take that as aggressive. Please can you tell me whether that is how you meant it?'

David fights when he feels that I am out of line on an issue.

Ernest gives me the satisfaction of telling me that he understands and then says, 'How could we help your boss to understand how difficult that would be for us?'

David tells me how desirable it is that I should settle the deal — how much be thinks it would be to my advantage.

Ernest tells me how very difficult it is for him to produce the settlement I must have.

David is of course very much the brighter of the negotiators. In fact I find him quite frightening. Ernest, on the other hand, is very amiable and he always leaves me feeling as if I am quite a competent chap. In fact if I am completely honest about it, I must admit that Ernest gets me to concede a lot of things where I would put up a brick wall against David.

The point of the story is that there is a great deal to be said for being relatively slow and painstaking, and encouraging Other Party to lead with the initiatives. Being clever does not win friends or influence people.

Apart from influencing the negotiator, we can also influence the situation.

We need to help the Other Party arrive at a potential settlement. For this we can offer:

— a different deal
— a similar deal but with conditions better for him
— readiness to consider offering better conditions, in return for offers from him
— different ways of valuing things
— a different plan/path towards a settlement
— issues packaged with one another in a new way
— a change in the shape of the deal
— a new opportunity ('Maybe we could handle installation?').

The situation is also influenced by the use of bluff and brinkmanship.

Competitive Parties each know perfectly well that the Other is to some extent playing a bluffing game. They expect it — they even respect the negotiator who plays that bluffing game to maximum effect. But there is always the risk that the game will be lost.

'Brinkmanship' is walking on the edge of the precipice. The seller who is demanding £50,000 for a bit of equipment may be facing a buyer who says he will not pay more than £40,000. If this situation has been reached after two or three rounds of bidding and bargaining, then one negotiator may feel tempted to go right to the brink. For example, the bidder may well say 'All right, if you won't come down to £40,000, then we won't buy one'. The seller does not know whether this argument is real or a bluff. There comes a time when he has to assume that it is a bluff and refuse to concede further. First Party cannot withdraw without losing face, and the parties go into deadlock.

There is always such a risk of deadlock in the process of competitive bargaining.

There is of course skill in using the bluffing game. It is needed whenever Other Party takes a position which we conceive to be so unrealistic that we ourselves have to go beyond our normal bounds. We cannot concede too fast or he will gain too great an advantage. What is more, if we concede too quickly then he will not value our concession as much as if we concede more slowly.

The manner in which we bluff must of course give no hint that we are bluffing. We must put it coolly and with conviction (despite the risks).

Reading the Other Party

How do we tell whether Other Party is bluffing? How do we know whether he means what he says, or whether he is just trying to gain a special bit of advantage?

There are some non-verbal clues (reference 6). I am more likely, for example, to believe the man who looks me straight in the eyes, than the shifty-eyed. I am more likely to feel for the man who says it with a smile, than for the one who is poker-faced. But I may be wrong, and given the lengths to which some negotiators will go and their skill in bluffing, I doubtless make mistakes.

Some experts are very keen on the non-verbal clues, and recommend looking for more subtle symbols (reference 10). For example, if you see Other Party crossing his arms, this is said to be a sign of resistance to what you are saying.

Then there is blink rate. Most people blink consistently between 4 and 8 times per minute. Under some circumstances, and particularly under stress, this blink rate increases, and some experts advise negotiators to pay great attention to such changes of blink rate.

This sounds a fruitful way to learn what the Other Party is thinking, but my own experiments show that observing blink rate is very arduous; so arduous that all one's energy is absorbed in making the observations. There is no energy left to hear what the Other Party is saying — one just does not hear a word. And then, even having noted differences of blink rate, one still is not sure how to interpret them. My conclusion therefore is that it is a waste of one's scarce energy to look for blink rate.

This is disappointing but seems to be part of a picture in which exaggerated claims are made for the value of non-verbal clues to what Others are thinking.

I remain convinced that we can communicate a great deal non-verbally — we can communicate mood, pace, enthusiasm, vigour, emotions — but we can also act. I am therefore unconvinced about the case for using a lot of energy on observing his behaviour.

The pattern of concession

The principles that govern concessions in bargaining are:

1 A concession by one party must be matched by a concession by the Other Party.
2 The pace of concession must be similar as between the two parties. If you give a little — then you must give no more until the Other Party has given a little in return.
3 We should trade our concessions to our advantage — doing our best to give him plenty of satisfaction even

with our small concessions.

4 We must help him to see each of our concessions as being significant.

5 Aspire high.

6 Move at a measured pace towards the projected settlement point.

That 'measured pace' must not concede too much too quickly; but on the other hand it must be sufficient to promise hope of reaching settlement.

Let us take an example. Suppose that (sadly) the two Parties had allowed a negotiation to degenerate into a head-on confrontation on price.

> Buyer offers £100,000 for a plot of land.
> Seller asks for £200,000.

After the initial round of bidding both parties see a predicted settlement area of £140,000. They assume that it will take a certain length of time — maybe four rounds of bidding.

Suppose first that as buyer, I am in a hurry. I can say, 'OK, I hoped to buy it for £100,000 but let's be honest, £140,000 would be realistic.' I have conceded too much too quickly.

The same would be true if I had even offered a first move to £120,000.

But I must not move too slowly either. With the parties so wide apart, a revised offer of £105,000 would have been derisory.

What then is a recommended pattern? A measured pattern of concessions would be:

> Round 1 — buyer offers £100,000
> Round 2 —   £114,000
> Round 3 —   £127,000
> Round 4 —   £135,000

Correspondingly, the moves from the seller would be:

> Round 1 — seller offers £200,000
> Round 2 —   £175,000
> Round 3 —   £160,000
> Round 4 —   £147,000

and both parties would then expect to shake hands at
£140,000 at the end of round 4.

We have suggested guidelines as to what concessions should
be made. There is the further issue of the manner in which
concessions should be made.
Guidelines are:

1   Reserve concessions until we need them.
    There is a jargon recognised by experienced negotiators
    to handle the situation when one of them could concede,
    but needs to keep the concession open for later trade-
    off. The phrase is 'OK, well let's leave that issue for the
    moment — I do not think it should prove too much of a
    stumbling block later on'. Respect Other Party when he
    makes that statement . . . . but of course make sure that
    we get the concession later on.
2   Trade readiness for readiness, match concession for
    concession.

    'Well it is extremely difficult for me to move at all on
    this price issue. If you could see your way to discussing
    the delivery issue, I suppose that might help us to take
    a new look at price, but as things stand, it would be
    impossible. How about the delivery issue? Can we
    discuss it?'

Breaking an impasse

How do we cope when the two Parties are a long way apart
and are refusing to go in for any kind of compromise? The
first guideline is of course to avoid such a situation if at all
possible. And this takes us right back to the skills with which
the opening and successive phases of negotiation have been
conducted.

But if we do find ourselves in deadlock then we need some
treatment for the real differences between us.

The principle underlying this treatment must reflect the
realities of human life and attitudes. People who really
believe in the stance which they have put forward for
negotiation, just will not readily yield on that stance. Partly

because the situation (in the sense of the enterprise which they are representing) has the right to expect them to sustain that stance; and partly because their individual credibility is at stake.

This 'individual' credibility is a form of the *face* of the negotiator. Negotiators strive constantly to preserve their face, their status, their credibility, to Others, and their self respect. We must constantly be seeking to ensure that the Other Party is able to make concessions without having to incur a loss of face. This means that the manner in which successive rounds of bargaining are negotiated must show that gain is being made by each party, towards an honourable settlement. There is no hope of success from ploys which seek simply to subjugate the negotiator of the Other Party.

But let us return to *real* differences of view which affect the results of the enterprise and not simply the face of the negotiator.

The first principle in coping with these conflicts is *keep it fluid*. We have previously described a negotiation on the subject of price as though price were the only variable. In general, price will be only one of several variables under negotiation. It may be of key significance to one Party but Second Party may not see it as having top priority. Second Party might really be more concerned about delivery. He might be prepared to trade an improvement in price for an improvement in delivery – and so to enable the parties to get away from the head-on confrontation on price.

This type of give-and-take is possible only when the parties have negotiated laterally (on a broad front): when each party has throughout put forward some sort of bid on all the issues (price, delivery, quality, terms, etc.). It is not possible when the bargaining pattern has become vertical, i.e. when the focus has been on one issue such as price, and when the price argument has been pursued to depths creating moods of conflict, aggression and excessive competition. So the first principle in dealing with real situational conflict is – keep it fluid.

The second principle is 'seek easy escape routes'. For example, negotiators may dive deeply into their conflict on prices. Each party may become committed to the point where deadlock is threatening. Yet conflict has easy escape routes available when it is only price that is in dispute:

- start talking discounts
- how about terms of payment?
- change of specification
- quality control
- rebates
- allowances for old goods
                    and so on.

Third, use time breaks. Either as recesses within a particular negotiation meeting, or as breaks between meetings. And on resumption (be it after a short recess or be it after a longer interval) re-start with the commended patterns of ice-breaking, opening with procedural agreement, moving into exploratory statements.

Even with such skills, conflict between negotiating parties can still lead towards deadlock. What are the rules 'if all else is failing'?

Firstly, all else does not usually fail very quickly. Experienced negotiators go very far along the steps already advocated before finding a need to turn to more strategic steps.

If all else really has failed, then it is helpful to change the mood of the negotiations.

One option is for team leaders informally to move out of the negotiating arena, into the 'Golf Club' sort of atmosphere. To move into some ambience in which informal discussion can take place within surroundings emphasising the elements of openness, frankness and integrity which can exist between the parties. Remote from the competitive pressures which have grown up within the negotiating room. Note in particular the possibilities of the team leaders having a refreshing meeting under these circumstances if they have not become personally involved in the battles of the negotiating room. If their style has enabled them to leave the wrangling to subordinates while they control negotiating processes. Second, try some changes in the team. Third, bring in the bosses from back home. Fourth, look to bringing in third party arbitrators or even third party chairmen to control further negotiation.

Towards a settlement

The Parties become aware that a settlement is approaching. There comes a new mood, a growth of vitality and energy as they sense the approaching culmination of their work.

At this stage there is a need for each party to make a final offer. Characteristic of this final offer are:

1 It should not be made too soon, otherwise it will be taken as just another concession — one of many still to be hoped for.
2 It must be big enough to symbolise closure. Rounding off a bid of £143,271 to £143,200 is not sufficient to symbolise closure. Rounding it off to £140,000 may be too generous but it would certainly have the required impact. But coming down from £143,271 to £142,000 would be interpreted as simply one step on the way to a natural settlement point of about £140,000. Your options are either £143,000 or £140,000.
3 When negotiating to our advantage demand the last halfpenny. If you do not squeeze the final ¼ per cent off his discount or the final two days off his delivery — he will not have the satisfaction of believing that he has taken you absolutely to the limit. Give him that satisfaction.

And finally, at the end of the negotiation:

1 Summarise.
2 Produce a written record.
3 Identify action needs and responsibilities.

Summary

Bargaining to our advantage, the skilled negotiator will:

1 At the outset ascertain the Other Party's needs, wants

and interest.
2 Assess the situation and decide how to handle it.
3 Prepare for each successive round of bargaining.
4 Influence the other negotiator – help him to achieve satisfaction and do not try to tread him down.
5 Influence the situation and the Other negotiators' reading of that situation. Bluff and brinkmanship have their part to play – risky though it be.
6 Concede at a measured pace and only in parallel with counter-balancing concessions by Others.
7 Keep the negotiating process on a broad front, and pay due attention to face and fluidity.
8 Avoid impasses.
9 Recognise imminent settlement; make a symbolic closing gesture, then see that the deal is written up and implemented.

After all this is over, the negotiator should have secured a deal which is to his advantage whilst at the same time giving the Other Party equal satisfaction.

At the end of it all, however tough it may have been, there will come a mood of companionship and of mutual respect between the negotiators. The tougher the negotiation the more boisterous the celebrations are likely to be.

But on the way to building skills as negotiators we are still far from finished. We need next to look at some more of the tactics which can be used to our advantage, and then to think of how to deal with fighting negotiators.

11 Tactics 'to our advantage'

Our underlying aim at this stage continues to be negotiating 'to our advantage', whilst at the same time offering the best satisfaction to the Other Party. To help us reach this objective there is a range of tactics which we can use occasionally. Some are new; others were mentioned in chapter 5 but should now be used differently.

For the new range of tactics, we shall consider:

- how each is used
- how Other Party reacts
- implications for the negotiation
- advantages
- disadvantages
- counter-tactics.

Feints

This involves focusing attention on issues not critical to ourselves, with the aim of enhancing their value in the satisfaction of the Other Party.

This is one of the most important tactics in the armoury for negotiating to our advantage. It enables us to give satisfaction and to sustain positive relationships with the Other Party, whilst still continuing matters to our own advantage.

If we think he is really concerned about price while our real concern is delivery — then a feint would be to focus on payment terms, so distracting him from both key issues.

Counter-tactics

Skilfully used, this tactic is difficult for the Other Party to counter. It can be a positive influence without serious risk of disadvantage.

'Lack of authority'

When the negotiator finds that he is being forced towards conceding more than he wants, he pleads that he doesn't have authority to complete a deal at the terms now being discussed.

This is a tactic constantly at the edge of any negotiator's repertoire. It is recognised by both Parties as being part of the normal manner in which 'the game is played'. As long as it is used in a veiled sort of way, it does not cause a disruption.

It is however disruptive to introduce the 'lack of authority' tactic in a more direct way. The conduct of a negotiation demands that the two Parties should together move towards a potential agreement point in a measured way; together trading, satisfying and conceding. A different problem arises when one party has no authority to do this trading. Second Party is then faced with the possibility that any understanding reached with the Others will not be approved by higher authority. Further concessions will be demanded.

Such lack of authority in Other Party is then a disadvantage to both of them. It disrupts and interferes with the pace and pattern of concession by Second Party. It holds up First Party's abilities to gain advantage. It makes the complex pattern of any negotiation even more complicated.

Such real lack of authority in Other Party is damaging to the effectiveness of the negotiating process. Used as a deliberate tactic, to fool the Other Party, it retains all the disadvantages and has the additional one – our unnecessary bluff may well be discovered to our disadvantage.

Counter-tactics

Negotiators are advised, whenever they fear that Others might use this tactic, to clarify the situation at the outset. Having established the purpose, plan and pace for the negotiation, and before entering the exploratory phase – that is, at the point where personalities are being introduced – raise the specific question: 'Do you have authority to settle this matter?'

If the lack of authority is pleaded when the negotiations have reached an advanced stage, then First Party should exert every influence to get an authoritative settlement. The Other Party should be offered telephone, telex and overnight accommodation facilities to enable them to check back with their principals and so to avert the authority obstacle.

Hawk and dove

In a two-man team, one member leads in the early stages of the negotiation and then hands over the leading role to his colleague for the concluding phases.

The advantage is that the team is now enabled to make very high demands at the outset, to state them firmly without any reservations. Then the stage is reached when the individual who has been making the demands cannot withdraw without loss of face: a stronghold position has been established which that individual (the hawk) must defend. On the other hand, the dove has remained quiet and can seek moves towards agreement – even suggest readiness to concede, without his personal 'face' being at stake.

The disadvantage is that this requires extremely close teamwork between the pair of negotiators; and each usually has more than enough to worry about without the additional problem of complicating the teamwork.

Counter-tactics

The tactic is difficult to counter. The Other Party must at
first concede very slowly − not retreating quickly in the face
of the hawk's threatening position. But then, when the dove
comes in, it is difficult not to over-react and to give way un-
necessarily because of his more reasonable approach.

Convert his objection to a 'yes-able'

Take the Other Party's hostile and very negative statement;
serve it back to him in a question to which he can only
answer 'Yes'.

The theory here is that His negative mood is interrupted
by His series of affirmative statements:

> 'I just will not pay that price.'
> 'Am I right in thinking you will not pay that price under
> any conceivable circumstances?'
> 'Yes.'
> 'That the price is impossibly high for you to pay?'
> 'Yes.'
> 'That this quality is not good enough for you to pay
> that price?'
> 'Yes.'
> 'That it would need a much improved quality before
> you could consider this price?'
> 'Yes.'
> And so on.

This is the sort of tactic which old Ernest Hargreaves
uses rarely, but David Crewe cleverly uses it a lot − and
infuriates people.

'Why?'

A constant demand for the reason − and for the reason
behind the reason.

> 'The most I can offer you is £1,000.'
> 'Why?'

'That is the most that will enable us to make any profit on the deal.'
'Why?'
And so on.

This use of the 'why' type of question is of positive value at the outset of the bargaining process. It helps us towards building our picture of what the Others really value.

It is part of the armoury of the way to ask questions which should be used at that stage.

Counter-tactics

We should offer only the essential information to give direct answers to the question. We should not elaborate beyond that immediate point – though, at the opening of the bargaining phase, Other Party has every right to press for the best terms he can get.

If on the other hand the Other Party introduces the round of 'why' questions, at every moment when we are trying to put forward new initiatives or to offer concessions – if he asks unreasonably for justification in the detail of every step, we shall become offended and aggressive.

Apart from this group of new tactics, there are also the different ways in which we can use some which we discussed in chapter 5 as 'tactics towards agreement'.

Recessing

This remains a positive tactic to use – and to use quite regularly. It gives both parties an opportunity to refresh their thinking and to take fresh stock of positions which are constantly changing; and to think out their tactics to gain advantage whilst still enabling both to feel satisfied.

The guidelines for using the tactic remain the same:
- state the need for a recession
- state the reason for it
- agree duration
- avoid fresh issues
- re-open with brief ice-breaking
- make fresh re-opening statement.

Setting deadlines

Again this is a helpful tactic enabling both Parties to move towards the phase in which the final burst of energy overcomes the obstacles, without the low energy which is shown in the middle of timeless negotiations.

'What if . . . .?'

This is an effective tactic which now takes on a fresh meaning. Instead of being used almost entirely in the exploratory phase, it now becomes a tactic for the bargaining phase. A tactic to be used when probing where Other Party's interests really lie.

> 'We could offer you 1,000 of these at £270 each at 8 weeks delivery provided we have cash on delivery.'
> 'What if we were to order 5,000?'
> 'Well, that would enable us to reduce the price fractionally, but it would not make very much difference.'
> 'What if we put up the order to 1,000 a month? How soon could you then make the first deliveries?'
> 'Oh well, that would be very different. We would have to tool up in order to offer you that much.'
> (Or maybe the answer could be quite different: 'That would be attractive to us. If you wanted to press on that front then we should be able to get the first batch to you quicker than 8 weeks.')

The 'what if' tactic is here being used effectively to gain an understanding of what is to Other Party's satisfaction during the bargaining phase.

Full disclosure

This no longer has the merit that it enjoyed when we were negotiating 'Towards Agreement'. We are now negotiating 'to our advantage' and we need to ensure that we obtain at least as much information about Other Party's desires and satisfactions as we give about our own. We need a measured pattern in which disclosures are at equal rates. We give away far too much if we ourselves offer full disclosure.

'All I've got is 60 per cent'

When negotiating 'Towards Agreement' this statement is used openly and truthfully, as a step towards identifying what is in our best mutual interest. The issue has become: What should we do together, subject to the limit of 60 per cent of price?

When negotiating 'to our advantage', the same question need not be absolutely valid. It is always possible to find a little more money, but the offer of 60 per cent enables us to get a better insight into the price situation of Other Party. A bit of bluff is part of this pattern of negotiation.

Lubrication

Just as important – just as significant.

The Golf Club

This is again a useful tactic. Even more so now that – negotiating 'to our advantage' – each Party is aware of dealing with bluffing games. Whether we know that Other Party is bluffing or not, we must always be suspicious. One way of resolving the inevitable doubts when an impasse draws near, is to withdraw to an environment within which we are most likely to be able to trust the integrity of the Other Party.

Summary

1 We need to use tactics which aim towards giving satisfaction to Other Party whilst at the same time

helping us to gain advantage for ourselves.

2 Such tactics include feints; pleading lack of authority; hawk and dove team game; the use of 'yes-able' questions; and the use of demanding questions ('why', etc.)

3 Still we need to use some tactics which we might have used if we were negotiating creatively to mutual advantage, but our use of them now seeks to shift the balance of the Other Party's satisfaction — in our favour.

12 Winning a fight

This book has so far concentrated on the skills found in two patterns of negotiating. First the skills in negotiating creative opportunities and moving Towards Agreement. Second, when creative possibilities are limited, the skills of producing that fair deal which gives equal satisfaction to both parties.

Negotiators sometimes meet another pattern, a head-on confrontation, a fight. They need to be prepared to cope with that pattern when they meet it and this chapter leads up to the skills they will need to display when coming up against a fighter.

On the way to discussing those skills, we need to consider:

1 When fighting methods are used.
2 Attitudes and objectives in fighting negotiations.
3 The pattern of a fighting negotiation.
4 Fighting tactics.
5 Counter-measures.

The use of fighting methods

The nature of a fighting negotiation is that one party should 'win' at the expense of the other. The aim is to win and to make the Other Party the loser.

The dangers of taking this approach are:

1 Forfeiting the goodwill of the Other Party.
2 Losing opportunities for more advantageous development in the future.
3 Provoking the Other Party to fight back — and the original aggressors may even lose.
4 A Party battered into submission is not likely energetically to implement any agreement.

These dangers are so intense that skilled negotiators will rarely use the amateur's fighting tactics.

There is however a rationale: two types of situation in which the fighting approach may not do too much damage.

First, the one-off negotiation, when the parties are not likely to come together again. There is now no concern for long term relationships.

Classic examples include (a) the doorstep salesman and (b) a privately arranged house purchase, without the niceties imposed by estate agents and solicitors who will continue to have to do business with one another.

Second, the situation in which one party is much more powerful than the other.

The great monopoly which could equally well buy from one of many competing suppliers; or the authoritarian state dealing with the private individual.

In those circumstances, we are wise to recognise that we may meet such treatment from an aggressive party. But there is no cause for us ourselves, when in the stronger position, to resort to fighting tactics. We can still retain the style 'to our advantage'. We can still expect to make a very good deal, and not run the risks of fighting.

But it is not only when there would be a suitable excuse that we meet fighting negotiators. Some people seem to be natural born fighters. Others seem to revel in the tricks and devices of fighting negotiations. Yet others are influenced by what they read in the media about negotiations, or the dramatic fare provided for them on the screen.

Do not go looking for a fight but do be prepared; be able to recognise the way the fighter works and be prepared to counter.

Attitudes, objectives and methods

The fighter's attitudes spring from his concern to dominate. He believes that power is important and that 'winning is what it is all about'. He is very task-centred and is not concerned about the effect of his methods on other people.

He sees the Other Party as 'opponents'.
His objective is to win and to make them lose.

The means which he uses are powerful. Both by his personal behaviour and by the negotiating tactics which he uses, he seeks to reinforce the power of his position. His methods include:

— a constant search for gain at every opportunity.
— at each successive stage in the process of negotiating, he wants fresh advantage.
— any withdrawals must be deliberate, tactical withdrawals, designed only to promote greater advance.
— power-methods: high in terms of the pace, size and forcefulness of demands, low in readiness to listen or to yield.
— task-centred. Concern for his special advantage. Not concerned with the Other Party's pride or dignity nor with their feelings. Forcing them to 'accept or else'.

Here then are the basic objectives and methods of the fighting negotiator.

The pattern of a fighting negotiation

The central concern of the fighting negotiator is to win. This winning takes place in the fighting phase of the negotiation — a special version of the bargaining phase. A special version at which he is expert and best able to use his personal characteristics. Quickly he leads the negotiation to the point at which his form of bargaining becomes the dominant activity.

This leaves little time or interest for the early stage of negotiating: little time to get on the same wavelength as Other Party, or to agree on a plan; little time to explore mutual interests. Even issue identification is hastened and the negotiation quickly becomes focused on his first chosen issue.

The pattern of the negotiation is then 'vertical', deep diving on the first selected issue.

He aspires high and pushes until he wins on that issue.

Successive issues are discussed, with the aim being to get a win on each successive issue. Settlement eventually is forced by him.

Fighting tactics

He knows a lot of tactics and manoeuvres, and regularly uses a number. He has his own repertoire, and admires (and tries to emulate) tactics which have been used 'against' him by other negotiators.

Here are some of the tactics he uses:

Probing from the start

The fighter enters the negotiating room, shakes hands and wishes us 'Good morning' and immediately starts probing. Probing about our business situation, probing about the product or service in which he is interested, probing about our own personal business situation:

> 'Good morning. How's business? How's the cash flow? Have you managed to get the quality put right yet? How are you getting on with the boss? What has been happening to your deliveries?'

The advantages he seeks are in getting information, in building a picture about Other Party and especially in re-

cognising weaknesses and vulnerabilities. Additionally, he
establishes a power position – a pattern of aggressive leadership.

Get/give

He is concerned to get something before he will give anything.
To get a small concession before he will give a small concession. To get a big concession before he will give a big concession. To get information before he will give information.
To get the Other Party's bid before he will give his own bid.
To get the power of being the first to make an opening
statement.

Get/give tactics used by skilled negotiators can have
positive commercial advantages in the short term. They may
well gain ground during the negotiating meeting. The disadvantages are that in the long term, they will introduce
the risk of delay and deadlock (neither party being willing
always to give before it gets).

Showing emotion e.g. anger

Loud and emotional statements, possibly banging the table:
the form of eye-contact, posture, gesture, and voice, all
displaying anger.

Good guy/bad guy

This is a tactic for use by a team of two negotiators. One
takes the role of the 'bad guy'; being aggressive, making
excessive demands, dominating, unco-operative. He holds
the stage for a long time whilst his colleague remains quiet.
When he has softened up the 'opposition' with his tactics,
the 'good guy' takes over the lead role, constructively
offering solutions, quietly trying to reach a mutual understanding.

The tactic parallels the archetype on which prisoners of
war were cross-examined; the prisoner first ruthlessly inter-
rogated by a tough investigator, then offered the sympathy
of a different personality to whom – with luck – he would
open up.

Poker-faced

Giving away nothing by expression, tone, posture or gesture. An important part of the fighting negotiator's armoury.

Managing the minutes

Taking responsibility at the end of each session for production of the record. Slanting interpretations of what has been agreed, always to own advantage. Readiness to include the odd items 'which ought to have been agreed' even if there was insufficient time to include it in the discussion. Provided, of course, that the odd item is favourable.

'That was an understanding not an agreement'

After making Others concede in the interest of reaching an agreement, going on to deny the finality of the agreement and to demand further concessions.

> Having moved far down the negotiating path, having enticed Other Party to concede — say to reduce his price of £1,500 and to settle for £1,200, the fighter comes back next day to continue the negotiation. He mentions at some stage a price of £1,000 and to our horrified response, 'But we already agreed on a price. We agreed on a price of £1,200', he replies, 'That was an understanding not an agreement.'

Getting upstairs

When unable to come to an agreement with a negotiator, taking steps to contact his boss, or boss's boss's boss.

The forcing moves

There are, of course, yet other moves which some negotiators use. Bribery, sex, blackmail, bugging. Most negotiators would see such devices as rankly unethical; but people negotiating very important deals are at risk and need to be on guard against such devices.

Counter-measures

The measures which we should be taking to counter the
fighter fall into four categories:

1 Head him off.
2 Control the battlefield.
3 Cope with his tactics.
4 Develop our attitudes.

The most satisfying way of coping with him is of course to
head off the fight before it develops. If this is to be achieved
it must be done in the critical opening seconds and minutes:

- deflect his opening questions
- preserve a neutral ice-breaking period
- do not be drawn by his probing questions
- do not let him assert leadership
- do not let him dominate the early moments — what is
being talked about, when to stand and when to sit, the
seating arrangements.

We are able to control the skirmishing if we can somehow
control the battlefield. In negotiating terms, this 'control of
the battlefield' is control of the procedures of negotiating.
Guidelines are:

1 Seek for form and plan for the proceedings.
2 Seek for opening discussion of purpose, pace and plan.
3 Keep bringing him back to the agreed plan.
4 Keep things fluid. Use the 'broad front' approach.
5 Seek for compromise. He will be impervious either to
searches for creative resolution of differences, or to
sensitive attempts to influence him. If his position is
that he is asking £120 and ours is that it is only worth
£100, then settlement is probable only at compromise
point, £110. Bargain slowly until you get him down to
at least £110.

Above all, keep control of the process — keep control of
what is being negotiated and in what sequence — keep to the
plan. It will irritate him. He much prefers to be able to run
free, but do not worry. A caged fighter cannot do as much

damage as one on the loose.

To cope with some of his tactics:

When he is using the 'get/give' tactics, we must not give way. If we give before we get, he will regard this as a sign of weakness and he will look for even more. He will want to get yet more and will change the tactic into 'get/get/give' and soon will be aspiring even higher to 'get/get/get'.

We must not give in. We must trade scrap of information for scrap of information; scrap of readiness for scrap of readiness; scrap of concession for scrap of concession.

The only counter to displays of anger is to suspend negotiations, either temporarily or permanently. The human brain is such that emotions (such as anger) are handled in one part of the brain; rational thinking in another part. Once the brain becomes focused on emotive thinking, then the rational part of the brain is cut off. The angry party cannot receive rational messages and it is no use Other Party trying to instil them. So the counter is to suspend operations. It does not matter to Other Party that the anger should be simply displayed rather than real anger. He has no way of being sure about the matter. First Party has behaved in ways which are not acceptable in negotiation and Second Party should immediately suspend.

The 'good guy/bad guy' tactic is difficult to recognise and therefore difficult to counter. But of course, if it has been recognised in one round of negotiating then we will be alert for it during later rounds and must hope either to be able to ignore the bad guy or to separate the two 'opponents'.

The counter to 'getting upstairs' is to state strong objection to the tactic and then to arrange for our own boss to come in and make it clear that theirs was a losing tactic.

Apart from such specific counter tactics, we have to develop our attitudes if we are to deal with fighting negotiators.

For one thing we cannot be sensitive either to his needs or to his reactions to us. He wants us to be. We cannot afford to be.

We must preserve calmness. We must avoid being forced into emotional behaviour or emotional reactions to his behaviour, however offensive it may be.

This sounds easy. It is not. His behaviour emphasises personality aspects which readily call forth a response in most of us. If he shouts, we are likely to shout back; and so on. Avoid it. Preserve calmness and rationality.

If he is pushing beyond the bounds of what we conceive as reasonable behaviour, then we should not sit with people behaving unreasonably. Get up and go.

If he seriously wants a deal with us, then he can come back at a later time. If he does not seriously want a deal with us, then we have nothing to lose.

Summary

1 Fighting of battles is not normally a recommended approach to negotiations.
2 Fighting needs a strong power base and a strong fighter.
3 War is no place for fine feelings.
4 The pattern of a fight leaves little time for opening niceties. Quickly the move is towards hard bargaining.
5 The fighting negotiator is usually a capable exponent of fighting tactics.
6 In seeking to counter a fighter:

  — try to head him off
  — control the battlefield — control what is discussed and in what sequence
  — keep it fluid, on a broad front
  — adopt counter-tactics
  — do not be sensitive
  — keep calm
  — be prepared to get up and go.

For further reading on tactics, see reference 5.

Finale to Part II

The aim in Part II of this book has been to review the skills needed when the negotiator is concerned more with gaining advantage for his own Party, less with creating the largest opportunity.

Key elements in this pattern are:

1 It is to our advantage to give satisfaction to the Other Party.
2 Preparation needs to include precise aims and targets.
3 Create a climate which is pleasant, brisk and businesslike.
4 It is still desirable to agree a plan from the outset — a plan which we can later use to control the negotiation.
5 Make the 'highest defensible bid', presenting it firmly, without reservations, without inessential justifications.
6 Get best understanding of what the Other Party wants and why; then analyse his real position.
7 Influence the situation and influence the other man — give him satisfaction.
8 Trade concession for concession, keeping things fluid ('on a broad front'), avoiding an impasse.
9 Use a wider range of negotiating tactics.
10 Fighting is not skilful negotiating.

Just as we offered a check-list of skills for negotiating

Towards Agreement at the end of Part I, so we now offer
a check-list of the skills for 'earning the advantage' (see the
facing page).
We suggest using the same procedure:

1 Take photocopies.
2 Fill in one copy, drawing up a profile of your own skills
   — what you're very good at, what you're not at all good
   at, and what lies in between.
3 With a different coloured pen, put in another profile, on
   the same copy: a realistic ambition of the skill level to
   which you might develop.
4 Get a couple of knowledgeable colleagues to draw up
   the other copies, and discuss with you their views of
   your actual and potential skills.
5 Decide what skills you need to develop.
6 Set down for each the specific steps you could take to
   improve.
7 Make a diary note for three months ahead, to check
   your new effectiveness against the targets you have
   set at step 5.

Second skills check-list

	Choosing bids	Presenting bids	Assessing others' needs	Helping others get satisfaction	Bargaining to advantage	Using advantageous tactics	Controlling the negotiating process	Sustaining goodwill
10								
9								
8								
7								
6								
5								
4								
3								
2								
1								

Part III

Towards mastery

Prologue

This book has so far been describing and distinguishing between the skills used in two different approaches to the conduct of negotiations. Mastery of negotiating also demands:

1 Skills which are needed irrespective of the approach.
2 Strategic decisions on the way a negotiation should be conducted.
3 Effective management.

Part III of the book considers those issues. First, when two or more negotiators are together representing one Party, they need special skills to work together as a team (chapter 13).

Chapters 14 to 16 are devoted to considerations of strategy and to the strategic decisions that should be taken. The considerations include the negotiating styles of the two Parties, the cultures of different countries, and some specific conditions for each negotiation.

Such strategic decisions are needed at the outset of important negotiations; and are part of the distinctive considerations for conduct of negotiations which are to take a long period of time (chapter 17).

In chapter 18, we move out of the realms of 'how to' and into the realms of 'why'. We look at elements of psychology.

This both justifies the distinction we have drawn between different approaches to negotiating, and throws fresh light on our conduct.

The negotiator's effectiveness depends in part on his own competence. It depends also on the situation created for him by his boss. Chapter 19 is on 'the management of negotiators', and looks at some key issues confronting the negotiator's boss.

Finally, in chapter 20, we discuss how the negotiator's skills should blend to give him strength and influence.

13 Teamwork

In this chapter we shall be concerned with the team; with choosing and organising the negotiating team, with choosing the team leader, with the way the team operates, and with the colleagues who remain at home.

Team selection and organisation

How big should a negotiating team be?

In one sense, the size of a team should conform to the old adage about the size of a commiteee – 'The best number of people to have on a committee is one'. The problems of ensuring collaboration, ensuring communication between team members, ensuring that each member has a satisfying element in the negotiation – all these problems of satisfying the team members can exceed the problems of negotiating with the Other Party. In the words of one highly experienced negotiator: 'When we were in Mexico we had a lot of trouble negotiating with the Mexicans. But that was nothing to the trouble I had with my own colleagues'.

But there is often need to have more information and more expertise available than any one person can contribute.

155

Commercial knowledge, financial knowledge, transport information, international experts. A case can be put up for a dozen or twenty people, each having a contribution to make within some major international negotiation; but if we take a dozen and the Other Party takes a dozen that is a total of twenty-four and obviously twenty-four is not a comfortable number to be negotiating.

What then is a commendable size for a negotiating team?

I suggest that the number is probably four. The main reasons for this number are:

1 Size of group.
2 Control of team.
3 Range of expertise.
4 Changing membership.

Size of group

There is a maximum size for a work-group such as a committee, if that work-group is to be productive and fruitful of ideas, everybody contributing; without that work-group growing too big for everybody to be involved, and too diffuse in the range of interests and ideas conveyed. That maximum is about eight people. In negotiation, we are concerned with a group which consists of two teams and the maximum of eight would be generated by two teams of four.

Control of team

For team control reasons four is also a convenient number. Management principles suggest that the span of control for any manager operating in such dramatic and changing circumstances as the conduct of a negotiation, is about three or four people. If the team leader is required to oversee the negotiations and the co-ordination of a team with as many as six or seven people responsible to him, then the team leader has too large a span to be comfortably controlled.

Range of expertise

The range of expertise required in a protracted negotiation, lasting over several months, may well need the contribution of a dozen or a score of different perspectives from each team. But within the scope of any one negotiating meeting, it will not be possible to take more than three or four different perspectives.

There may be need for more detailed discussion than can be handled by the leader and three or four members. For example, a production member may not have sufficient detailed information on production plans, material supplies, technical feasibilities, etc. and may need the support of specialists from those fields. When this happens, it is normally possible to arrange a sub-negotiation: for a separate work-group consisting of the production member from each team, together with three or four specialists assisting each, to meet as a separate group, independently of the main negotiation. The respective specialist members will report back to the main negotiation.

Changing membership

There is no need to keep the same team throughout. As negotiations develop, the need for particular forms of expertise changes. For example, production and technical expertise may be invaluable in exploratory and creative phases, but redundant when it comes to the legal embodiment of settlement. Equally, the presence of lawyers who should be concerned with details of drafting is a positive encumbrance to members at the creative phase of a negotiation. It is not necessary for the team membership to remain constant – the production member might well be present for the first three or four meetings in a series, leaving a seat vacant for the next couple of meetings, and bringing in a lawyer for the final couple.

There are then reasons to suggest that four should be regarded as a maximum size for a negotiating team. If there is need for more people to be present at a negotiation – for example, if further experts are needed – they should be there in the role of advisers to the members who are negotiating and not as full members of the team. They should, literally and metaphorically, sit behind the members.

In making this assertion that four is a convenient number, we are considering genuine patterns of negotiation. We must distinguish nominal patterns in which groups of possibly a dozen people are required to act as a team. Such patterns are found, for example, within the jurisdiction of some governments. Where such governments are involved in commercial negotiations the apparent formalities are conducted within the forum of teams of twelve but in these circumstances real patterns of negotiation tend to take place outside the formal negotiating room.

Key people are needed at the negotiating table. In the selection of teams for negotiating there is always likely to be conflict between this need for key people to be involved in the negotiation, and the need for the same key people to keep things running back home. This is a managerial problem and priorities need to be set by the bosses of the negotiating team.

However, the case for key people being included in negotiating teams does not rest solely on the contribution which they will make at the negotiating table. It rests also on the degree of commitment which these key people will feel for the results of the negotiation. Commitment to implementation is highest when such key executives have been involved in the negotiations, and feel a sense of ownership of the results.

Specialists and experts, however brilliant in their own field, are often strangers to the world of negotiation. If they are to be effective supports, and especially if they are to participate as negotiating members of the team, they need training to cover:

1 The presentation of information.
2 Negotiating tactics.
3 Teamwork — both role handling and support of colleagues.
4 Rehearsals, which should include exposure to tough opposition if that is the style which Other Party is expected to adopt.

Always, the individuals selected for any particular

negotiation should be welded into a team before meeting with Other Party. This requires a discipline of preparation and the creation of understanding between team members.

To summarise:

1 The size of a negotiating team should be limited to a maximum of four members.
2 If more experts and specialists are needed, they should attend as observers and advisers to full members of the team. They should not have a speaking brief.
3 Key people may have to be assigned from their other duties within the enterprise, not only to carry weight at the negotiating table but also to give them 'ownership' of decisions and of subsequent implementation.
4 Experts and specialists need training just as much as negotiators.

The team leader

Who is the ideal leader of a negotiating team?

The calibre of the team leader is important. He or she must be seen to be of the same calibre as the team leader of Other Party. Without equal calibre and the abilities to deal on the same level, Our Party will soon become subjugated by Other Party, leading to defensiveness, counter-aggression and the risk of being over-powered.

But beyond that question of calibre there is no single style of leader who is, in all circumstances, to be preferred to any other style. What is important is that the team should work together effectively, and team-effectiveness depends upon the members being able to operate in a style to which they are accustomed. If they are in an enterprise where all information is fed to one boss, who then takes all the management decisions — then the negotiating team needs a corresponding sort of leader. One who will bear the brunt of the discussion during the negotiation, turning to his team members only for advice to him about situations and possibilities within their special interest, which he will then pass on. If, on the other hand, the enterprise is one with a style including much delegation, the team leader needs to be one who will control the negotiating process with a loose rein, encouraging his team members to make major contributions.

The style of the team leader needs to reflect the style of the enterprise from which the team comes, and there is no one style which is always 'right'. Nor is there any particular discipline which is ideal background for a team leader. The role may be found among production people, marketing people, or financial people. It is most likely to be found amongst people of commercial experience; less likely to be found in those with technical expertise. As a rough generalisation, experienced negotiators seem most often to come from those who have spent their formative years in the hustle and bustle of the commercial world, rather than university graduates.

Team support

Team members should support one another both verbally and non-verbally.

At the very start of the negotiation, there is a potent influence from the way in which the team leader introduces his colleagues.

> One team leader introduced – 'Our accountant, Norman Kellett'. At another negotiation, the leader introduced – 'Norman Kellett, who has fifteen years' experience in handling the financing and the financial control of projects up to £15 million.'
> Norman Kellett was noticeably more influential in one negotiation than in the other.

Throughout the negotiations, there is a need to ensure that each person's statements are reinforced by his colleagues.

Verbal reinforcement by such comments as 'absolutely correct' and 'Yes, that is right'. Verbally further reinforced by statements from one's own perception which support the original statement.

> The production man's comment about delivery problems

— 'I am afraid all machines are fully booked up for the
next three months', reinforced by the marketing man's
comments, 'Yes, and I am afraid too that the order
book is continuously full so that even three months will
be terribly difficult.'

However obvious such support may seem, it is neglected in
far too many negotiations.

Principal: 'Well if you really expect us to pay that much
for a pump, we will just do without one.'
His Technical Adviser, to him: 'But we have got to have
one.'

It is not only verbal support that is important between
team members. It is also non-verbal support.

When Tom and Harry go out together regularly to
conduct negotiations, Harry becomes used to what Tom
says every time. Good old Tom — he goes on for ten
minutes talking about the technical qualities of our
nuts and bolts. It is always the same story and Harry
has got bored by it. He concentrates his eyes on the
paper in front of him and his thoughts on yesterday's
golf. It is natural for Harry to do so. And it is natural
that the Other Party should see Harry treating Tom and
Tom's statement as old dead beat.
Then there comes the day when Tom goes out with
Jack instead of Harry. Tom makes exactly the same
series of statements but as he does so, Jack shifts his
chair a couple of inches so that he faces more towards
Tom. He watches Tom intently, he nods his head
approvingly at some of the statements. He looks across
at Other Party to check that they are giving their full
attention to Tom and are recognising that they hear
the words of a man of great experience and wisdom.
Tom, with Jack, is more influential than when he's with
Harry.

The back-home team

The negotiating team will need the support of the people back in the enterprise. These will in part include bosses, to whom we turn our attention in a later chapter. They will also include peers, secretaries and subordinates.

The negotiating team may well need to negotiate with this back-home team before setting off. They will need to check on the extent to which they can commit the organisation and commit their colleagues informally as well as formally. They need to communicate and involve the back-home members so that they can expect support whilst they are away.

There is further a need to recognise the probability that there will be conflict between any away-team and the back-home team. This type of conflict has been systematically researched. It will inevitably grow between the home and away teams unless positive steps are taken to prevent it. The only steps which have been shown to work require eyeball-to-eyeball contact between the two teams — the away and the back-home. Possibly by the negotiating team returning to base for progress discussions with colleagues. Possibly emissaries either from the negotiating team or from the home-team repeatedly visiting the other.

Summary

1 Teamwork depends on the size and selection of the original team.
2 It depends on a team leader of the right calibre, operating in ways which are familiar to team members.
3 Members of the team should support one another both verbally and non-verbally.
4 Liaison with the back-home team requires face-to-face contact both before and during the negotiations.

14 Different styles of negotiating

The skilled negotiator, regularly meeting many Other Parties, recognises that each has its own distinct way of negotiating. He attunes to the differences, and adjusts his preparation and his conduct.

In the next two chapters, we shall examine differences of style which reflect the ways in which different organisations work; and then, differences of negotiating related to different countries and cultures.

Task-centred or people-centred?

One classification of organisational style (reference 2) distinguishes between people who are task-oriented and people who are people-oriented.

People who are purely task-oriented are concerned entirely with achieving a business goal. They are not at all concerned about the effect which their determination will have on the people with whom they come into contact. They will pursue their business objectives relentlessly; they will go to the limits of morality; they will, as negotiators, be very tough, very fighting, very aware of tactical ploys and anxious to make maximum use of them.

People-oriented managers on the other hand, are highly concerned about the well-being of those who work for them, or alongside them or above them. This concern about people dominates their activity — says the theory — and it can lead to an almost total neglect of the business goals. Such an intensely people-oriented negotiator would of course be a 'soft touch' for the task-oriented Party.

The same theory recognises that there are intermediate points between total task-orientation and total people-orientation. It splits this central area into three parts:

1 Low-orientation both to task and to people.
   But of course such low achievers would hardly be expected to reach the status of negotiators.
2 Medium-orientation both to task and to people.
   This centre group is characterised by the continual search for compromise. Given that seller asks £100 and buyer offers £80 there is always a search (focusing around £90) for compromise between the parties.
3 High-orientation both to task and to people.
   This style is characterised by forms of behaviour prized by psychologists. Tremendous openness and trust in forms of relationship. Great forethought, 'getting sound creative decisions', 'seeking out ideas, opinions and attitudes different from one's own'.

When one analyses the teachings of this school of thought, one again recognises three styles of negotiator one is likely to meet in practice:

1 The fighter — highly task-oriented.
2 The collaborator — aiming to get everything into the open, confront issues and make a creative deal.
3 The compromiser — looking always to compromise to settle deals.

These three distinctive styles of negotiation are thus styles which we can associate with different sorts of organisation. So what? How should this influence the way we conduct our negotiations?

First, we must recognise that the different patterns of behaviour are deeply ingrained in the people we are likely to meet. They will tend naturally to follow their set ways of doing things. They will not easily adapt to our approach.

If therefore we want to adopt an approach different from theirs, we must understand and build the distinct skills of that approach. We must become the more skilled negotiators – more skilled in 'doing it our way' than they are in 'doing it their way'. This sort of skill can only be gained through experience and feedback – either through the feedback we may be able to obtain from colleagues after we have negotiated as team members, or through the compressed experience of practical training seminars in which we can get feedback not only from colleagues but also from the 'Other Party'.

Second, we must take account of the Other Party's style in our preparations. The most difficult situation is when we want to negotiate 'Towards Agreement' or 'To Our Advantage' but we anticipate meeting skilled fighters and fear being beaten. Then we must prepare our defences; and those defences must include preparing for ourselves bids and tactics which will give us ample room for manoeuvre.

It is an unfortunate consequence of this preparation that later, when we meet the Other Party, we will have low concern for exploration with them. Having prepared in this way, we will have a high degree of readiness to put forward our bids, and subsequently to defend them and to use the tactics we have thought about.

In other words, the form of our preparation to meet skilled fighters will have led us to contribute to the development of the battle. More positively, if we anticipate meeting skilled fighters but have confidence in our own skills – if we are not afraid of being beaten – then our preparation and conduct of the negotiation will not need to be based on preparing our defences. Our preparations now can be restricted to obtaining a clear definition of purpose and aims, without yet going hard on our opening bids, and our targets for the first phase of negotiation can be restricted to:

1 Establish a negotiating climate and procedure which

suit our style.
2 Give and get opening statements, confined to general remarks on hopes and fears for the negotiation.
3 Seek for control of the procedure and style.
4 Break to review and to prepare for next phase of negotiation.
5 Re-assess Other Party's style and skills.

Personal flair or systematised?

Other theories (e.g. reference 11) distinguish between personal and bureaucratic styles. One element of such theories again reiterates the desirability of a style corresponding to that which we have described as 'Towards Agreement'. Other parts of the theory draw our attention to two different categories; the 'pioneer' and the 'bureaucrat'.

The 'pioneer' is the strong individual. Prominent in his own organisation. The sort of man who is good at seizing an opportunity, spotting a market, making a profit. He tends to be a very dominating personality, good at improvising, intuitive in his thinking, charismatic in his personality.

A negotiator of this type will be pushful, forceful, ready quickly to take decisions and to come to agreements. He will be distinguishable particularly in the way in which he acts as team leader: the focal point of the team, the one who speaks for the team on all issues, the one who uses his team members to obtain information for himself which he then transmits to Other Party.

Such a team leader, though he usually bubbles with energy, is even so able to handle only the content of a negotiation. He cannot at the same time have conscious concern for the procedures of the meeting.

Advantage might be gained by Other Party – not only for itself but for the whole of the negotiation – if their team leader could keep his energy concentrated on the process of the negotiation, leaving his subordinates to handle the content issues. But in practice the 'pioneer' is so powerful a character that it takes somebody with similar stature to maintain a dialogue with him. That is, it takes Other Party's own team leader; and that other team leader is then absorbed in the whirl of content issues.

Given sufficient prior knowledge that they are about to meet this 'pioneer' negotiator, Other Party can shape their preparation accordingly.

Some of the issues to which they will need to attune are:

1 The need to choose a team leader of corresponding personality.
2 The need for own team leader to be highly briefed. (The 'pioneer' team leader knows a lot about the detail of issues — much more than a team leader who practices delegation.)
3 Team work will require that team members are constantly alert to feed team leader with facts and figures. They will need to help the leader during the negotiation as the Other Party 'pioneer' develops and demands attention.
4 A team member should be nominated to take over the role of concern for the procedural development of the negotiations; prompting and helping his team leader to control the plan and development of the negotiation.
5 Party will need frequent recesses to consolidate its own information, in response to the flow of details which will come from the 'pioneer' negotiator.

Negotiating with a 'pioneer' can be exciting, enjoyable and highly productive. It demands however that we should recognise his highly intuitive, instinctive nature. That we should not seek to confuse him with excess of rationality. And yet that we should ourselves retain a consciousness of the negotiating processes through which we are going, trying to sustain our normal degrees of control.

Bureaucracy is the pattern most often found in large organisations. The style of working is systematised. There are books of rules, standardisations, planning, numerous committees. Lots of checking, double-checking and cross-checking. The organisation is governed by a clear hierarchy, compartmentalised and co-ordinated by the system, the rules, the procedures and the objectives.

Advantage within a bureaucratic organisation comes to

the people who are most competent at playing the game according to the rules. This means that their negotiators may be expected to have both objectives and styles of working which are bureaucratic.

For example, in setting up a deal, the objectives of the bureaucratic negotiator may be strongly influenced by the way in which that deal will be fitted into the budgetary provisions. Fitting it into that budget may be, for him, more important than the total sums of money involved.

> Once, in negotiating a contract with a bureaucrat, I received a lot of preliminary correspondence which I assumed was an attempt to force me to reduce a quotation. When we finally met he said that the budgetary limitation was about one-third of the price I wanted. So I stood up to go, and he then said: 'But of course there is another budget' which could produce up to another one-third. And by the time my jaw had dropped and I had sat down again, I was learning that there were very many parts to the budget. Throughout, his interest was and had been, not on the issue of price, but on the issue of how the total could be distributed around various parts of the budget.

Not only differences of goal but also differences of manner in negotiation. Stylised bureaucrat, formal i's to be dotted and t's to be crossed. Precise statements to be agreed at each step as we go along the negotiating process. Elegance and conformity in the way in which the records are maintained.

In anticipation of meeting with bureaucratic negotiators, Other Party does well to select a team which has both the personality and experience to handle this manner of operating. The team will find that the bureaucratic group will readily accept the *system* of approach we have advocated to negotiations; it will, for example, follow the procedural discipline of agreeing purpose, plan and pace. Its behaviour will be impeccable. But the *attitude* of looking together for joint advantage does not come easily to the systems-minded. They see two sides to be represented by the negotiating parties, not one group of two parties working towards agreement. Bureaucratic organisations thus tend to have distinctive objectives, and to negotiate in the pattern 'to our advantage'.

Which style wins?

I am often asked: 'Which style wins?'

The opening answer must be: 'Different styles produce different sorts of benefit'. A good American negotiator will get 51 per cent of the cake. But a good Norwegian negotiator will ensure that it is a bigger cake than it might have been.

When two Norwegians negotiate together, then they seek to build the biggest possible cake. The product of these negotiations tends to be a better situation for both parties – in which each side can be said to have 'won'.

When two Americans negotiate together, then it is the more skilled of the negotiators who will 'win' – even though he should at least give the Other Party the impression that they have not 'lost'.

When a skilled collaborative negotiator meets an unskilled competitive negotiator then collaborative processes will dominate the negotiations.

And when a skilled competitive negotiator meets with an unskilled collaborative negotiator then it will be the competitive who dominates.

This is to take us into the aphorism 'horses for courses'. The party which is skilled, and in particular the party which is skilled for the particular situation, the party which is capitalising on its innate strengths, this is the party I should want to negotiate for me.

But finally we come to the issue – when skilled collaborator meets skilled competitor – who wins? I do not know. I think that if each party had the skill to recognise the strengths of the other, and to work with the other to the point at which that form of skill was most important, then we could expect a superlative outcome; but I suspect that this is asking too much and that we would get dominance by one party or another.

Summary

1 Different organisations work in different ways; and each has a characteristic style of negotiating.
2 A first distinction is between fighter, compromiser and collaborator.
3 Negotiators need training and experience before they can successfully handle the differences of style of Other Parties.
4 There is need to anticipate the style of the Other Party and — especially if they are believed to be aggressive — to prepare to deal with that style.
5 Preparation of strong defences helps to breed battles. A negotiator with skill and self confidence will seek for control of the climate and the procedures in the opening phases: not for putting forward his own defensive/aggressive position.
6 'Pioneer' negotiators operate with a lot of personal flair, and tend to dominate.
7 'Systematised' negotiators are distinctive both in their manner of operation and in the goals which they seek.
8 No single style of negotiating 'wins'. It is the more skilled negotiator who will prevail.

15 Differences of culture

Let us now switch from looking at the distinctive features of organisational styles to looking at the distinctive features which we can associate with different countries.

People from different countries have different values, different attitudes, different experience. They have different strengths from one another and different weaknesses.

In my view the competent negotiator should develop a style which is appropriate for his own strengths — including the strengths of his particular culture. He should not seek to follow the style of a different culture — he should not follow a style in which other people have strengths which he does not have, a style which would lead to displaying his natural weaknesses rather than his natural strengths.

He needs to become aware of what those strengths of his are and to practise the skills of exploiting them.

He needs also to be conscious that other people operate in different ways. It is important to respect their different ways without being subservient to them.

For example a detail of the way in which Arabs communicate with one another is that they will have different physical contact from that of Western Europeans. Possibly a linkage of fingers, possibly a facial contact. But Arab negotiators are suspicious of Westerners who adopt these gestures. They respect the Other Party which — whilst itself respecting Arab traditions — retains its own courtesies.

The differences of national culture not only influence such superficial behaviour, they also condition the underlying values held by negotiators. Each person brings to the negotiating table deep-rooted assumptions of which he may not even be conscious.

In the remainder of this chapter we seek to bring into the open some such underlying assumptions and practices. Not the least significant of these distinctions is between the American and the European approaches to negotiation.

American

The American style of negotiating is possibly the most influential in the world. It is the style which dominates the literature and one which many other people seek to emulate.

It is characterised first by personalities which are usually outgoing, and which quickly convey sincerity and warmth. Personalities which are confident and positive and which readily flow into exuberant conversation. The negotiator enters the negotiating room confidently, talking assertively.

Within the American culture, great respect attaches to economic success. There is a great tradition of wheeler-dealing. There is concern to acquire the symbols of material success.

The American negotiator, enthusiastically starting negotiations, appreciates this attitude of the search for economic gain. His strengths are particularly high in the bargaining phases of negotiation. He naturally moves quickly towards those phases. His ways of 'playing the game' assume that other negotiators should be governed by the same set of rules. He respects those who are the most adept at handling the bargaining processes and those who play the game by the same rules. He is himself adept at using tactics to gain advantage, and expects others to have the same professionalism.

With those attitudes, focused on the bargaining process,

the American negotiator is interested in 'packages'. A seller
expects the buyer to be able to give him a statement of the
package which he requires; a buyer expects the seller to
come with a clear package. And I deliberately use the word
'package' because it implies a little about the product, and
a lot about the manner in which that product is presented.

There are then four characteristics which we have here
identified about the approach of the American negotiator:

- exuberance
- professionalism
- bargaining ability
- interest in packages.

In part, it may be that these characteristics can be traced
back to American history, to the pioneers seeking a new form
of living, risking a great deal in extending the frontiers,
heavily influenced by the commercial instincts of their
Jewish population.

German

The German style shows quite a lot of difference. In particular the German preparation for negotiations is superb.

The German negotiator will identify the deal which he
hopes to make. He will identify exactly the shape of that
deal. He will identify the issues which he thinks should
enter into the negotiations. He will then prepare a reasonable bid, carefully covering each issue in the deal.

During the negotiation, he will put the issues and the bids
clearly, firmly, assertively.

He will not be significantly open to compromise.

The pattern of negotiating is surprisingly akin to some
interpretations of the German character. Thorough, systematic, highly prepared, low in flexibility and compromise.

It is a very powerful style when practised by skilled
negotiators. Its strength rests particularly in the bidding
phase of negotiations. Once enunciated, the bids seem to
take on some degree of being sacrosanct, so that the scope
for bargaining is diminished.

How to cope? Procedurally it is desirable for Other Parties
to ensure that exploration and their own opening statements
are introduced before these bids are tabled. They can thus
bring into the picture their own perspective, but they have
to be sharp to do so since the German negotiator is so very
good at his own preparation and since he moves so naturally
and so speedily into the bidding phase.

French

French negotiators are reputed to have three main characteristics in international dealings: a great deal of firmness,
an insistence on using French as the language for negotiation,
and a decidedly lateral style in negotiating. That is, they
prefer to make an outline agreement, then an agreement in
principle, then headings of agreement, and so on, repeatedly
covering the whole breadth of a deal; in contrast to the
American piece-by-piece approach. And, like de Gaulle, they
have a high capacity to gain by saying firmly 'Non'.

English

The English are seen by other nationalities to be:

- amateur, as distinct from American professionals
- under-prepared rather than over-prepared
- kindly, friendly, sociable, agreeable
- flexible and responsive to initiatives.

North European

The North European approaches negotiations much more
quietly than either the American or the German. There is
a degree of reticence about the way he enters into social
involvement at the beginning of the negotiations. He is quiet
and speaks slowly and can easily be overwhelmed in these
early phases.

He is very open in his statements; he readily helps Other

Party to gain information about his own position.

And he is very good at spotting creative possibilities and reaching creative decisions.

Finns and Norwegians conform closely to this sort of pattern; Swedes also conform to it but have been more highly influenced by Americans and by the Swedish bureaucracy. Danes tend to be Scandinavian in style if they come from Sealand, and German if they come from Jutland.

The background reasons for these characteristics, at any rate in the Scandinavian countries, are not hard to perceive – Christian ethics, political stability, agricultural and fishing economies until relatively recently. The strengths of the North European are his frankness and openness during the exploratory phases of negotiation, leading towards his highly creative abilities in the next stage. He does not rank with either the Americans or the Germans as a bidder nor with the Americans as a tactical bargainer, but he can still be appropriately stubborn.

To respond: readiness with him to explore, to be flexible, to be creative.

Mediterranean

The Mediterranean culture is altogether warmer.

Warm greetings and social aspects. Exuberant uses of postures and gestures. Difficulty in pinning discussions down to particular deals or particular phases of negotiation.

In some regions, deals need to be 'lubricated'. Indeed, this question of 'lubrication' is central to the cultures of some Mediterranean countries. It is seen as a normal practice and does not have the repulsive character (to North Europeans) of 'bribery'.

The approach to negotiation in these cultures needs to retain the types of discipline we have been discussing; and yet to be conscious of the need for lubrication. Since no respectable western company would wish to be associated with the practice of bribery, the need is to secure a local agency and to ensure that that agency handles the lubrication.

Communist

The Communist approach is normally bureaucratic, sometimes with political overtones.

The bureaucratic aspects lead to a group of people being involved in negotiating. They have commitments to budgets, procedures and objectives which would normally be unknown to the negotiator from a different culture; and whose significance it is difficult for that negotiator to appreciate.

Methods, as well as goals, are bureaucratic. There is the protocol, systems, rules, procedures of bureaucracy to be followed.

This, for some Communist countries, is overlaid by the political system in which it is not uncommon to have a political representative amongst the negotiating team, checking on the conformity and performance of the remaining team members. Nor is this to be despised where the community — in the form of the State — takes full responsibility for economic matters. Then the interests of the members of the community — the individual workers — demand that there should be checks on the performance of those who can most influence economic success.

The negotiators under these circumstances have a security concern which is not known in Western society. Their ability to retain their jobs depends on their success from one negotiation to another — on the reports which are made on them — on the nature, the form and the force of their behaviour during the negotiations.

How to cope? Anticipate:

1 Heavy preliminary traffic, probably including specifications.
2 Changes in the shape once the deal gets under discussion.
3 Strong efforts to whittle down bids offered to them (a process of whittling down as distinct from bargaining).
4 The use of bureaucratic devices such as the manipulated minutes of a meeting.
5 Settlements highly detailed in writing; and a need to continue the negotiation through the drafting of the settlements.

6 The need to have the signatures of all who have in any way participated in the negotiation – and usually at least one more.

Middle East

The negotiator in the Middle East comes from a desert tradition. A tribal tradition in which there are close and compact communities. A desert tradition in which hospitality is a governing force. Time is not of the essence. Trust is extremely important, and the visitor must earn that trust. The Prophet Mohammed was a warrior and retaliation is more respectable than compromise.

The consequent patterns of negotiation put very high emphasis on the early phases of negotiation. Social aspects – an extended form of the climate forming/ice-breaking – last for a long time. Within that dominantly social period, some occasional aspects of the exploratory phases are taken into discussion – albeit often obliquely. From this extensive, social, mildly commercial discussion, may occur mutual respect and may emerge mutually acceptable realisations of commercial possibilities. Then suddenly, deals can be agreed.

But be prepared first for delays and interruptions. The door is always open, and even when negotiations are at a critical stage they may be interrupted by some third party coming in to discuss some totally different topic. He will of course be made welcome in the best Arab tradition.

The inexperienced European negotiator is likely to be thrown off balance by this loss of momentum. He must develop the skill to adapt to this pattern, to accept the relative timelessne·s, and to be able – when the right moment comes – to lead the discussion back and to rebuild the momentum.

The pattern then is one of extreme emphasis on the climate formation and the exploratory phases which we have discussed in the negotiating process. At its most effective, this traditional Middle Eastern pattern can largely circumvent the bidding and bargaining phases on the way to a settlement.

This traditional pattern has to some extent been overtaken

by the oil revolution, with increasing numbers of Arabs being exposed to American patterns of education and influence and absorbing the American approach to bidding and bargaining.

Indian

The Indian loves the bargaining — the market-type haggling — and feels deprived if negotiations do not include a suitable bargaining ritual.

Chinese

The Chinese negotiator is distinguished by:

- concern for 'face'
- specialism
- suspicion of Westerners.

The 'face' issue is most important. He must be seen to be negotiating with someone of key status and authority, someone whose Director's visiting card is elegantly presented, someone with a car of substance and a driver properly uniformed. He must not be forced to lose face by having to withdraw from a stance firmly stated during negotiations — nor can we sustain our all-important face with him if we withdraw from a firm statement. The final agreement must be one which enables him to sustain — or preferably improve — his face as perceived by his acquaintances.

The specialisation means that there will be lots of experts at the negotiation. The technical expert, the financial expert, the shipping expert, and another three experts. Inevitably this leads to protracted negotiations, each expert establishing and safeguarding his face during the negotiations; and I know one exporter who budgets one man-day of negotiation time for every £10,000 of business he hopes to do.

> It's a useful rule-of-thumb. It means for example, two men for a week to negotiate a £100,000 deal; a team of five for a month for £1,000,000.

The Chinese are suspicious of Westerners. Especially they resent Western attempts to lead them into political discussions. More positively, the Chinese welcome genuine interest in their families. A present for the son (a small present that has had some thought put into it — not something ostentatious) is precious — in contrast to a big business lunch, which is worthless.

Summary

Every culture has its own distinctive approach, and in looking at a range of cultures, we have identified a range of different approaches to negotiation.

We suggest that it is important for negotiators from each culture to develop their natural strengths, rather than to adopt approaches which would inevitably expose their weaknesses.

When they meet other cultures, they should respect and promote — but not be subservient to — the negotiating customs of that culture.

16 Strategic decisions

The purpose of this chapter is to help the practical negotiator to decide on the strategies he will follow in his negotiations. It will therefore cover:

1 What strategic decisions are needed?
2 On what grounds should they be made?
3 Guidelines on how to make them.
4 Specific examples.

What strategic decisions?

The key issues which need to be considered outside the negotiation itself include:

— With whom — with what Other Parties should we negotiate?
— How high should we aim?
— What sort of objectives should we set?
— What style should we negotiate in?
— What team should negotiate for us?
— What special problems and opportunities exist?

Decisions on these strategic questions will, of course,

vary from situation to situation; so we shall now look at the causes of one situation differing from another. What are the considerations we need to have in mind when forming our strategies?

Strategic considerations

There are half a dozen background considerations which will influence our strategy:

- repeatability
- strength of Other Party
- strength of our Party
- importance of the deal
- time scale
- negotiating resources.

The question of *repeatability* is an important influence on the style and tactics we should use. If we are carrying out a whole series of deals with one organisation, then we need to build goodwill and lasting relationships with that organisation. We get to know one another personally – maybe our respective golf teams have an annual match – and we evolve a pattern of the way we negotiate together.

If, on the other hand, we are negotiating a one-off deal with an organisation we are not likely to meet again – at any rate, not for a long time – then the situation is strategically different. We are not necessarily bound by the same concern to establish goodwill. Nor is the Other Party.

The first strategic consideration, then, is the repeatability of the deal.

The second is the *Other Party's strength*. This strength is partly a matter of their situation. If they are the only people with whom we could possibly do such a deal, then they are in a strong position. If, however, we have many potential customers (or suppliers) then they are in a relatively weak position.

The Other Party's situation also includes the style in which they operate, and the personalities who negotiate on their behalf. Both the style and the personalities should influence our choice of strategy.

Their strength is an important strategic consideration. So is *Our strength*.

Our strength is the converse of theirs. We are strong if we dominate a market — either as buyers or as sellers — weak if we are just one of many. We too have a style characteristic of our organisation, personalities and strength on which we should capitalise.

Three other significant considerations also apply during most negotiations.

There is the *importance of the deal*. If we are negotiating a deal worth millions of pounds, then our strategy needs to be different from negotiations in thousands of pounds. Or if we are negotiating a deal for a well established product in a well established market, we have less strategic concern than if we are at the dramatic point of launching a new product into a new market.

The *time scale* for the deal may also influence our strategy. If it is imperative that we conclude a deal quickly, then our negotiation strategy may be different from what it would be if there were little urgency.

And our *negotiating resources* may also influence strategy. If we have few negotiators of quality and many projects to be negotiated, then we cannot spare our negotiators for long periods on any one deal.

These are not the only strategic considerations. Each organisation, for each negotiation, will have some special concerns and considerations of its own. There will be issues which that organisation needs to take into account. We cannot generalise about those special situations, however, and for the moment we must concentrate on the above — the general considerations which will influence our choice of strategy.

Guidelines for strategic decisions

The first of the strategic decisions which we must make is the *choice of Other Party*. If we have any choice in the matter, how many Parties should we negotiate with? Which

Parties should we choose?

If we deal repeatedly, then we shall want to sustain durable relationships with people who do business well with us. This means limiting the range of people with whom we negotiate to three or four.

For practical purposes, if we have to continue extended negotiations, then 'three or four' is likely to be too big a number. We cannot easily conduct, control and compare complicated negotiations with as many as three or four enterprises. The most is probably with two – and in any case, others will not put great effort into negotiating if they know there are four parties in the field, so that their chances are only one in four.

It is desirable, however, to have some basis for comparison, and a general guideline for repetitive deals is to negotiate with two Others.

For one-off deals, we are not bound by the same concerns. The general strategy here should be to invite tenders, to make the first choice, 'in principle', on the basis of bids submitted; and then to restrict subsequent detailed negotiation to one Other.

The choice of which Other will of course be strongly influenced by the range of commercial interests. The reputation, the reliability, the integrity, the quality and so on of the possible Other Parties. It should be influenced also by the style and characters of the Other organisation. If we naturally negotiate best in (for example) the style of brisk bargaining described as 'to our advantage', then we shall be most effective when bargaining with Others who have the same sort of style. We shall not march happily with people who spend more time in exploring before getting down to the key business.

And conversely, if our strength is in being creative, we do best to work with people who are themselves creative and responsive to our own initiatives.

Second, *how quickly* should we negotiate? Do we want to get into the negotiation room, make a Quick Deal and get out again? If so, we need a strategy of opening the bidding very close to our minimum requirement.

Or have we ample time for negotiating? Should we Hold

Back? If so, we have possibilities of exploration and creativity; and possibilities, too, of opening the bidding at more optimistic levels and sorting out a deal with better advantage.

Marsh (reference 8) recommends:

> If we are the stronger party ('Dominant') — we should choose 'Quick Deal'.
>
> If we are the weaker ('Subordinate') — we should choose either Quick Deal or Hold Back, dependent on the strategy assumed to have been selected by opponent.
>
> If there is no clear pattern of Dominance/Subordination, we should Hold Back.

Third, *how high should we aim* in our strategic thinking? The general answer is that we must always aspire high.

The point was made earlier, in chapter 9, and exemplified by reference to a case study in which different negotiators, aspiring differently, obtained widely different results. Yet differences of aspiration would not — in everyday circumstances — be known to negotiators' bosses: they might guess, but could never be sure, that a negotiator's aim had been high or had been low.

It thus seems that their level of aspiration should be a key element in the selection and appointment of negotiators.

At any rate, the level of aspiration is a key strategic element in the conduct of any particular negotiation. Practical experience and psychological advice are unanimous; 'aim high, aim high, aim high', and so we earlier advised opening with the 'highest defensible bid'.

'Defensible' of course, taking into account the situation and what is reasonable for the situation; taking into account whether our strategy is Quick Deal or Hold Back; and taking into account, too, the pattern of our relationship with the Other Party and our understanding of that Party's negotiating style. But, with due deference to all these necessary reservations, always aiming high.

Fourth: *what sort of objectives*? The word 'objective' is in fact used to mean a lot of different things. There is a hierarchy of objectives, each level of the hierarchy being more or less general, less or more specific.

I find it helpful to distinguish three levels in this hierarchy of objectives. From the bottom upwards, the three levels are:

1 *Targets* — specific statements of intent to be achieved within the short term. For example, 'to have gained a clear understanding of the Other Party's offer'.
2 *Aims* — a slightly more generalised statement of the objectives for the next series of sessions, 'to have secured an order at a profit margin of 15% within product range X and size range Y'.
3 *Purpose* — an overriding and more general level of concern, 'to secure sufficient orders to take up the full capacity at (Blank) factory during the year 1985'.

There is a need strategically to decide how precise or how general we want our objectives to be.

For a Quick Deal, we need to have very precise targets, and very clear views about the extent to which we could compromise.
Despite the opinions of many experts, I do not accept that targets should also be precise when starting a Hold Back negotiation. I believe that such precision then acts as a psychological barrier, and curbs our ability to explore creatively.

Fifth, *what style* should we decide to negotiate in? Should we aim to operate creatively with the Other Party towards establishing a deal excellent for us both? Or would that approach be suspect — would it leave us too vulnerable? Or is there little scope for creativity and would we do better to concentrate on getting best advantage to ourselves?

If we have adopted a Quick Deal strategy — then we shall need to move quickly and our style should be 'to our advantage'. If we are Holding Back, then we have the options — either creative oriented or advantage oriented.

Then our choice should depend on what we are good at.
As we have previously seen, each enterprise has its own distinctive character and its own distinctive style of

negotiating. That style of the enterprise is in turn influenced by the culture of the country in which it exists. The individual negotiator reflects style of company and culture of country as well as his own individual character.

In the short term, each negotiator has his own strengths, and it is desirable that he should negotiate in a style which reflects those strengths. If he tries to adopt a style foreign to him he will only expose his weakness and is unlikely to get a good deal.

But if repeatedly we find that our style is not the ideal we would choose, for each normal strategic situation − then clearly we have a training problem with our negotiators. We need to equip them to operate in a different style.

This style decision is an important one, with its implications for the way we open our negotiations, for our targets in them, and for our orientation to exploration, to bidding and to bargaining.

It is also an important influence on the next strategic decision − the selection of our team. We need a team of a size and composition which is appropriate, as discussed in chapter 13. We also need a team which will operate in suitable style for the strategic situation − including suitable style to meet the strengths and the character of Other Party's team.

Finally, strategically, every deal will have special problems and opportunities. We cannot generalise. They must be matters for the commercial judgment of the negotiating team.

Specific examples

In this section, we are concerned to apply the analysis of strategic considerations to some specific situations.

Let us look at four different situations:

1 Buying
   Important deal
   One-off
   Buyer dominant
   Competitive suppliers
      This is a classic situation
      Obtain tenders

Choose the most attractive
Restrict detailed negotiations to that one.

2 Repetitive situation
Us dominant
Large orders
Competition amongst Others
Negotiate with at least two parties
Follow our natural style
Insist on doing so by careful use of 'control of the
negotiating process'
Aspire high.

3 Repetitive (but not identical) deals
Parties of equal strength
No alternative Other Party
Hold Back strategy
Evaluate Others: check whether responsive to a
creative strategy
Team selection should be influenced jointly by the
possibility for creativity and by knowledge of the
Other Party.

4 One-off deal
Equal strengths
No alternative Parties
We now have the same potential for creativity as in
number 3, but less risk in adopting advantageous or
even fighting tactics.

Summary

The considerations which determine the strategy we should
adopt are:

1 The repeatability of the deal.
2 The strength of the Other Party's situation, its style and
personalities.
3 The strength of Our Party's situation, our style and
personalities.
4 The importance of the deal.

5 The time scale.
6 The negotiating resources.

These considerations will influence our decisions on:

1 With whom should we negotiate?
2 How quickly?
3 How high should we aim?
4 What sort of objectives?
5 In what style?
6 Who should negotiate for us?

There will also be strategic considerations peculiar to each negotiation. Possibilities and opportunities which are unique and which must be identified for each deal by the negotiators — or their bosses.

17 Conducting extensive negotiations

The early stages of this book were concerned with the conduct of negotiations, without much concern for the length of those negotiations.

Distinct issues arise when handling major negotiations which are likely to last over an extended period of time. In this chapter, we look at these issues of extensive negotiations under three main headings:

1 The preliminaries.
2 Conduct of the negotiation.
3 After the negotiation.

The preliminaries

Before there is any move towards negotiation, Our Party must see some possibility of a deal being necessary and/or desirable. Once that possibility is perceived, and the matter seems to be one of considerable significance – possibly justifying extensive negotiation – then we suggest that there should be nine main steps in advance of the negotiations themselves.

1 Determine the strategy to be followed: consider the

191

form of the negotiation (one-off/repetitive), the
strength our party will have in negotiations, and the
nature of prospective Other Parties (dominance, sub-
servience). Together with importance of the deal, the
time scale of the deal, and the availability of our own
negotiators, we now have a view of the issues which will
determine our strategy.

2 And so we come to source selection. Who do we want
to be Other Party? With how many other Other Parties
do we need to negotiate on this issue?

3 Team selection. Leader, key members, experts and
occasional members.

4 Next, team organisation: to establishing the job remit or
the job specification for the team, team training and
preliminary meetings between the team and back-home
supporters.

5 The team itself will need to assess the objectives in the
light of their own brief and to prepare assessments of
the Other Party or Parties. This will involve the assem-
bling of documents both relating to the project to be
handled and all the information which can be acquired
both about the other enterprise and about the other individuals and the way they operate.

6 From this information, the negotiating team moves
into its detailed preparation for the negotiations. Again,
we advocate the same broad approach of first brain-
storming and then analysing.

The brain-storming is now a group exercise, in which
each member of the group should become involved,
and should resolutely avoid challenging the suggestions
of other members or discussing in depth. Step 1 in the
brain-storming is to collect thoughts on the sub-
ject-matter; step 2, on the Other Party.

Thereafter, the team together should analyse the
situation. A team may need a lot of time to agree a
simple thesis sentence; but that time will be amply
repaid in their later cohesion when they are face-to-
face with the Other Party.

They should also develop aims and targets for the
early phases of the negotiation; an outline schedule

for the total duration; and a note of the more detailed responsibilities for preparation which will fall on each team member. The greater the extent to which the backhome team can be involved in this series of preparations, the greater the probability of good collaboration in later stages.

7 We suggest a *phased* approach to preparation. That is, we do not attempt to prepare for every eventuality before we start negotiating. We prepare only that which we need to; and then prepare afresh before each successive phase in the later negotiation.

How much do we need to prepare at the outset? It depends on our 'strategy' and on our 'style' decisions.

If we are aiming 'Towards Agreement', intending a creative approach, then we need to keep our thinking as general as possible for the early stages of negotiation. On the other hand, if we are to be confronted by another Party operating with only their own profit in mind, then we need to insulate ourselves in advance so that we cannot be over-influenced by any extreme opening bids which They might put in, even at an early stage. For this purpose, we would need, at maximum, to have developed clearly defined 'targets', and at minimum to have put numbers into our more general 'aims'. How then should we reconcile these different needs: on the one hand to restrict to general statements so that we can start creatively, on the other hand to be specific so that we will not be exploited?

If our strategy and style are agreement oriented —
    Before the first round of negotiations, the team should have a thorough discussion and should write down the purpose of the whole negotiation, the thesis sentence — and the aims and targets should be discussed as hopes without committing them to paper.
    After the first round of negotiation, the strategy — and particularly the style 'Towards Agreement', — should be reviewed.
    After the exploratory and creative phases, review again and now develop specific aims, targets and

bids.

On the other hand, if strategy and style are 'to our advantage' — then from the outset, build in the numerical statement of minimum requirements and of concession lists ranging progressively from maximum to minimum.

8 Physical preparation is another necessary preliminary: booking accommodation and travel; scheduling rest periods; scheduling face-to-face contacts with the back-home group; arranging for communications with them and if necessary for coded exchanges of information.

9 In the final stages of preparation, it is desirable for the team to have a rehearsal, using colleagues to role-play Other Party. Testing both the plan for the negotiations and the manner in which the team will operate.

And so, fully and carefully prepared, the team is ready to move into negotiating with the Other Party.

Conduct of extended negotiations

The fabric of extended negotiations follows the same basic pattern as we have already discussed for negotiations as a whole. The establishment of climate and procedure, joint exploration, bidding, bargaining and settlement. Again, there are possibilities of approaching vertically (piece-by-piece — the approach more likely to bring confrontation) or laterally (the stage-by-stage process — offering the better chance of co-operation). And again, with demands for communications and teamwork during the negotiations.

With extended negotiations however, there is a further need: the need consistently to review progress and to make fresh plans. The reviews should daily cover:

1 Content of the negotiations.
2 Procedural development.
3 Team effectiveness.
4 Maintenance of climate.

By content we mean the topics under discussion — the

goods, services or activities being debated. What progress is being made? The reviews should take place against pre-conceived standards: that is, in comparison with objectives defined before each round of negotiations. They need to refer to the general purpose, defined before the negotiation started; and to the aims and targets which were defined either before the start of any negotiations, or in the preparation periods between successive sessions.

The review of content development must also cover any need to re-prepare and, in particular, to modify and develop ideas about the shape of the deal; and subsequently to confirm or modify bids and concessions. Targets for the next round should be defined.

By *procedural development* we mean the effectiveness of the planning and the pacing of the negotiations. This covers:

1 What progress is being made in moving through successive phases of negotiation?
2 To what extent is re-scheduling needed?
3 Would there be advantage in switching as between vertical and lateral sequence in negotiation?
4 Is appropriate use being made of recessing?
5 Should there be distinct discussions with Other Party to review progress and to re-plan or re-schedule the subsequent pattern of negotiations?
6 What communications are taking place with the back-home team and to what extent do these satisfy the team's needs for information and support — and the back-home team's needs?

Team effectiveness demands periodic reviews of the way in which our team is operating. For a team operating under a pioneering leader the key consideration is that leader's own feelings about the way in which his colleagues are operating.

For a more democratic team it is helpful to consider a wider list. One authority (reference 13) puts forward half a dozen characteristics which might well be assessed by the team at progress meetings:

1 *Goals* — are the team members clear about the goals we are pursuing? Do they agree about them?

2 *Participation* — are all team members involved? Are all effective?

3 *Support* — do all members back up one another? Both verbally and non-verbally?

4 *Feelings* — are the team members prepared to talk with one another about their feelings? To what extent are feelings being expressed to the other team and is that level of expression an appropriate one?

5 *Diagnosis of group problems* — when the team comes up against problems do they simply treat them superficially or are they probing them in depth?

6 *Leadership* — are needs for leadership being met by the team leader in his relationships with the team? By the team leader in his relationships to Other Party? By individual team members in taking initiatives when they have special expertise?

7 *Trust* — do the team members trust one another? Do they freely express negative reactions without fearing reprisal from colleagues?

8 *Expertise* — is the expertise within the group adequate? Is there a need to bring in fresh expertise to support team members?

Finally the daily reviews need to cover *maintenance of climate*.

The negotiating group consists of the two teams. Like all work groups, the negotiating group develops its own life-cycle and its own momentum.

Momentum and climate are created at the outset but must be sustained throughout the negotiation. Some of the guidelines for 'group maintenance' therefore come into play.

1 There must be a sense of purpose and achievement within the group. In particular it is desirable that both parties should feel that challenging areas are being negotiated and that adequate progress is being made.

2 Each party to the negotiation needs to feel that it is playing a worthy role. It is neither clever nor productive for either party to be forever in the lead, pushing, taking initiatives, hogging the dialogue.

3 Each individual needs to have a sense of belonging, a

feeling that he is contributing to the work of the group both as an individual and as a team member.

How to sustain these 'group maintenance' processes? Sustenance depends on the manner in which the group processes were originally handled: in part the ice-breaking but more, in having established a unified sense of purpose, plan and pacing at the outset.

During the conduct of the negotiations, progress should be repeatedly summarised, and repeatedly the continuing agreement between the parties should be made prominent:

'Well, gentlemen, we agreed at the outset that our plan would be to take the four steps A,B,C, and D. We agreed some while back that we had successfully completed A and that we should concentrate next on B. Can we agree that we have successfully completed B?'

And then, assuming a positive response, 'Can we then, as we agreed, move on to C?'

The team's feeling of worth requires that each team should give and take during the negotiation. In particular, it requires that each team should be playing a role both in determining the procedure being followed and in the content. The taking should include the acceptance of Other's procedural and strategic initiatives as well as winning points of substance in the bargaining process.

The alternative to this process of give and take is that one Party acquires a power position and continuously dominates procedure, dominates initiatives, dominates the bargaining processes. Such domination wins a short term advantage, but in the long term it arouses resentment and eventually hostility. The worm turns to the disadvantage of the power party.

Climate also covers the goodwill which is built up through a negotiation meeting. Goodwill does not rest on woolly concessions but on fair dealing about matters perceived to be difficult.

The critical impressions carried forward from any negotiation meeting are the final impressions.

Just as the opening seconds and minutes in a meeting are

of critical importance to the negotiations that are about to start, so the final phase is critical for goodwill after the meeting.

This development of the climate is an important element of the effective conduct of negotiations and justifies a separate item in the daily review processes. Daily review processes which, to summarise, should cover:

1 Progress in the content of the negotiations, reviewed against pre-determined standards.
2 The establishment of new standards for the next round of negotiation.
3 Procedural development – the planning and pacing of the negotiations.
4 Team effectiveness. The way we are operating.
5 Maintenance of the climate.

After the negotiation

At the end of difficult negotiations there is often a mood of euphoria. The tough brutes who were seen to be sitting on the other side of the table become close friends with whom one has achieved a mighty breakthrough to common advantage. Congratulations and celebrations!

Back home, there are immediate needs: the work need to start implementing the negotiations and to catch up with the pile in one's in-tray; and the personal need to rest, recuperate and restore domestic relationships.

These priorities are such that teams rarely give time to what they could be learning from the negotiations they have just completed. However, there is much to learn and a strong case can be made for a post-negotiating critique. Such critique should cover:

1 Our strategies – choice of Other Party, level of objectives, team selection, team style.
2 Our conduct of the negotiations – preparation, procedural planning, process control, scheduling.
3 Our team – authority and responsibility within the team, climate formation, training and development

needs, liaison with back-home group.
4 The Other Party — style of working, effectiveness as a team, effectiveness as negotiators and key concerns for them.

Summary

The conduct of extensive negotiations has some special needs:
In the preliminaries,

- determine the strategy
- choose the sources
- choose the team
- organise the team
- define objectives and gather information
- detailed preparation
- physical preparation
- rehearsal.

During extended negotiations, reviews to cover:

- the development of the content of the negotiations
- progress against pre-determined standards; and the establishment of new standards.
- procedural development — the planning and pacing of the negotiations
- team effectiveness. The way we are operating
- maintenance of the climate.

After the negotiations, critique:

- our strategies
- our conduct of the negotiations
- our team
- the Other Party.

18 Psychology in negotiating

This book has been concerned largely with 'how'; with methods for practical people to use during their conduct of negotiations. In this chapter our attention is more on 'why'; on looking at the underlying reasons which make sense of the methods we have suggested.

The chapter is in three parts:

1 To justify and give new insights into the distinctive approaches:

   – agreement-oriented
   – earning advantage
   – fighting.
2 To identify some of the different characters we may meet at the negotiating table.
3 To consider the application of recent theory:

   – to the development of our own negotiators
   – to helping Other Party to become receptive.

Justifying the distinctive approaches

One of the key theories about 'People at Work', is Maslow's

'hierarchy of needs' (reference 9).

Maslow suggests that human beings take actions in order to satisfy essential needs. He classifies human needs under five main headings:

Physical or survival needs
Our most important need is to survive, to remain alive. To remain alive, a man must have food, water, shelter and rest. So long as needs, upon which health depends, go unsatisfied, a person shows little interest in the other four types of need. His thoughts and energies will be directed towards satisfying the survival to the exclusion of all other needs.

Security and safety needs
Once the human being's most important physical needs are satisfied to at least a minimum and continuing degree, the next need that becomes dominant is the security or safety need. His efforts are now aimed at being comfortable, safe and secure. Security includes not only the physical safety of his person (locked doors and barred windows), but also includes economic security – a steady job, life insurance, a savings account, etc.

Social needs
When the individual is no longer continually hungry and has sufficient security, then 'belongingness' becomes most important to him. He needs to belong and be accepted by a small intimate group – his family and a few close friends and colleagues. He needs to receive as well as give affection. He feels the need to be wanted and accepted not only by his family but also by the group of people with whom he works and his other social groups, e.g. his church group, his bowls club, his work mates.

Ego or esteem needs
The individual whose physical needs, security and belonging needs are satisfied becomes concerned with esteem: that is, the need for self-respect and respect from others.

Self-realisation needs

If the physical, security, belongingness and esteem needs are all satisfied, the individual's most important need becomes self-realisation. This need is aimed at self-fulfilment; his desire to become his best self; to realise his capabilities to the fullest. This need is sometimes called the 'creative' need.

The successive levels of need are shown diagrammatically in Figure 18.1.

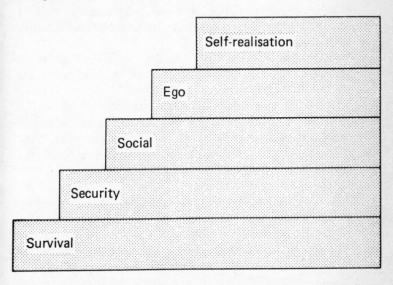

Fig. 18.1 Maslow's hierarchy of human needs

There is one further important element to Maslow's theory. It is the assertion that each lower level must be satisfied before people become concerned at a higher level. For example, they will not be concerned about the social need – the concern to 'belong' with other people – unless they are already satisfied that they can survive and are secure.

What is the relationship of this theory to the practical business of negotiating?

First, in order to reach the most advanced level which Maslow suggests, the creative level, the negotiators must first take care of the previous four levels.

In Part I of this book, we advocate firstly taking steps
which enable the negotiators to get at ease with one
another. Steps to ensure that the *survival* requirements
of room and refreshment are provided; the creation of
an atmosphere which is not threatening to the *security*
of either party; and that in the ice-breaking period, a
good *social* atmosphere is established between the
parties.

The next stage — the procedural agreement stage —
reinforces that social level and moves towards meeting
individual needs.

But *ego satisfaction* depends more on what a person
values, deep within himself, than on what we can create
within the negotiation.

If the individual values openness, frankness, creativity —
then he will be attracted by the suggested approach
'Towards Agreement'. There is every prospect that the
parties together can move towards operating on Maslow's
highest plane. Every prospect of substantial creative
agreement.

The disciplined approach towards agreement therefore
needs to be the basic process regularly used by the
skilled negotiator.

But at the same time he must check that the negotiation
is moving successfully through the lower planes; he must
ensure that it is not prejudiced by the security or ego
needs en route towards creativity.

Second, even when the survival, security and social needs
are met, there are many individuals whose values do not
include openness, frankness and creativity.

For them, the ego need has to be satisfied by material
goods and by respect.

The material goods are in the situation — in the package
or product to be negotiated. This negotiator is looking
for the best share he can get out of the deal.

His need for respect is a need for respect from three
different sources.

He needs the respect of his colleagues back home. If he sets off to the negotiation with clearly defined objectives, then it is important to him to go home with those clearly defined objectives duly realised. He must then pursue those objectives – they are fundamental to his personal satisfaction from the negotiation.

He will also be influenced by the respect of Other Party and where his value system emphasises material goods, then he will believe that Other Party's respect depends on his success in earning those material goods.

He will also be concerned with his self-respect. And his self-respect equally will focus on his success in winning material goods.

That is to say that this negotiator's approach is focused on 'getting what he wants'. He will negotiate effectively at this level, provided that early steps are taken to look after the survival, security and social needs. But it is not going to be possible to conduct the negotiation at the creative level at the top of Maslow's hierarchy. For these conditions, our strategy needs to be one of earning advantage. We must seek to give him satisfaction, of course, whilst we are earning this advantage. We must seek in our negotiation to increase the value he puts on items which we can concede; to lessen his valuation of items which we cannot concede.

Third, the inexperienced negotiator will not pay sufficient attention to the ground work.

He will dash into the negotiation and start quickly on the content. He will fail to provide the basic survival and security conditions, let alone to provide for the social needs.

These will create the conditions for aggression, defensiveness and counter-aggression; the basic conditions for hard fights.

To summarise: Maslow's 'hierarchy of needs' marches closely with the distinctive approaches in this book, respectively 'Towards Agreement', 'gaining the advantage' and 'winning battles'.

To identify different characters at the negotiating table

Another theory (reference 7) distinguishes people's ego needs as being in three categories:

1 Achievement. The need to produce results.
2 Affiliation. The need to relate to other people.
3 Power. The need to exert influence on people and situations.

Using this analysis, it is possible to analyse different individuals and to see how they will behave at the negotiating table. Let us take three fictitious examples:

Len Barnes. Len's needs are:

      — high for achievement
      — low for affiliation
      — high for power.

Len will go flat out to achieve what he thinks is important. This will not necessarily be the same as what his organisation thinks is important — he is low in affiliation needs and therefore in his need to satisfy the wishes of his boss or his colleagues.

Curiously, Len may not aim very high. Some achievement oriented negotiators even set themselves deliberately low targets, so helping themselves not only to achieve but to over-achieve.

Len's approach is powerful. He hustles for the best advantage, jostling for the sense of influence over the other parties.

How should we negotiate with Len? We can meet a lot of his power needs by enabling him to take precedence. Let him make the first statement and let him feel the ascendancy which that gives him. But at the same time we must tactfully keep control of the process, holding to our need for a clear plan and sustaining that plan through the negotiation.

If his achievement orientation has led him to set himself low targets, then we should not have much of a problem. We can let him reach those targets, but must ensure on the way that there has been sufficient of a battle that he can go away with the sense of a battle won.

Barry Walker. Barry Walker's needs, on the other hand, are:

- high in achievement
- high in affiliation
- low in power.

Barry, too, will be keen to go home with results which he regards as highly worthy.

But Barry's need for affiliation makes him much more responsive to the urgings of his boss and his colleagues back home. He will be concerned to go back with a result which not only he, but they, too, will regard as worthy. He will also be more concerned about having good relationships with the Other Party's negotiator.

His orientation to affiliation but not to power means that he will be more ready to be subservient during the negotiating process.

If we send Barry to negotiate with a similarly minded personality, we can confidently predict that they will go out together the following evening to celebrate a highly creative and satisfactory negotiation.

If we send Barry to negotiate with a power oriented person, the results will depend on how well we have trained Barry and on how well trained the other man is.

If Barry is the better trained, then he will use the steps of the negotiating process to achieve a satisfactory result — though he will not much enjoy having to combat the power minded party.

If, however, the power party is the better trained, then he will dominate the proceedings and the most we can hope for is that Barry will escape without having committed us too far.

Mike Garbett. Mike Garbett's needs are:

- medium achievement
- medium affiliation
- medium power.

The distinctive feature about Mike is this balance between affiliation and power. It is extremely rare to find people who are high on both power need and affiliation need — the power need is hostile to the possibility of keeping genuinely good relations with other people.

Mike, however, has distinct needs — medium needs — both for affiliation and for power. He wants to influence but not to dominate.

He can be expected to establish good relationships with the Other Party and to be responsive to the needs of his organisation and of his colleagues back home. He can be expected, too, to handle the negotiating process forcefully, imposing his will both on the content of the negotiations and on the process by which they are conducted.

Mike also has a need for achievement which will not be satisfied unless he goes home with results which both he and his colleagues will find satisfactory. (Satisfactory, not necessarily brilliant.) He will be prepared, if forced, to make a compromise. He would sooner have a satisfactory deal than no deal at all. Compare the high achievement negotiator, who would sooner break off negotiations, rather than settle for the merely satisfactory.

Mike has the potential to be one of our best negotiators. It is well worth ensuring that he is well trained to make use of his talents.

A recent theory

A major new contribution (reference 12) to the literature on motivation appeared in 1978. I am indebted to Dr. Sven Söderberg for the following summary and for his suggestion of the implication for negotiators:

> Salanick and Pfeffer argue that our attitudes and needs are built up from three sources, i.e. from our perceptual judgement of the present situation, from our relative

success in behaving towards a need-fulfilment, and from social influence and social information coming from other sources.

The model states that behaviour is a result of social influence, of how we choose among possible behaviours in a given situation and our history of relative achievement in a given sphere of behaviour.

Our relative behavioural achievements become part of our perceived social reality and our relative achievement feeds back into our set of attitudes and refines them. This later process is performed through attributing our relative success to either characteristics within ourselves (generally in success-type operations) or to characteristics outside our control (generally when we fail to reach our objective).

As I understand that theory, I conceive that its application to Negotiation suggests the following premises:

1 The level (of results of a negotiation) towards which negotiators can aspire is not fixed by the situation or by any agency outside the negotiating team. (Including their bosses in the team.)

2 The level at which any negotiator aims in a particular situation is determined in the first instance by his own attitudes and needs. These derive from innate personal characteristics, heavily influenced by his training and experience as a negotiator.

3 The/his team is further influenced — heavily — by the climate/attitudes/levels of aspiration of his colleagues and of his organisation.

4 Those 'home-based' factors set the level of aspiration with which he will approach a negotiation. But, within moments of entering the negotiation, he will instinctively make some (small?) revaluation, based on his perception of the mood/attitudes/personality of the Other Party.

Such an interpretation suggests the following actions:

1 Aim high.
2 Train subordinates to aim high.
3 Set a climate in your organisation of 'aim high'.
4 Let the Other Party quickly see that you aim high.

Summary

1 The approach to negotiating, 'Towards Agreement', is the most mature approach but depends on great skill in establishing the base conditions.
2 Negotiating 'to our advantage' demands the 'influence' skills of helping Other Party to be satisfied.
3 Fighting is a more primitive form of negotiating. When we meet unskilled negotiators, we need skill to help them to overcome basic fears, such as their security needs. But unless we are successful in doing so, we must expect a fight.
4 The assessment of negotiators — both our own and Other Party's — can be helped by use of achievement/affiliation/power analysis.
5 Recent theory underlines the need to aim high and to let others be aware that we aim high.

19 The management of negotiators

This chapter is intended for the senior manager, the boss of the negotiator. It looks at some of the key issues which concern him in his role and in his relationship with the negotiator. These issues are presented as falling within three categories:

1 Personal management — the selection, motivation and personal development of the negotiator.
2 Relationship management -- defining objectives and controlling the relationship between manager and negotiator.
3 Organisational management — the relationship between boss, negotiator and back-home support team.

Personal management

The key aspects of personal management are:

— choosing the negotiator
— training him
— motivating him.

First, the *choice* of our negotiator.

The selection criteria must cover four groups of factors:

1 Technical knowledge — of the product and of the market, technical or financial issues which will concern him during the negotiation.
2 Personal characteristics — a range of character issues. For example, the following are characteristics I would like to see in an effective negotiator:

  — aspires high
  — good presence
  — creative
  — articulate
  — good listener
  — determined
  — disciplined mind
  — high tolerance for frustration
  — dispassionate
  — enjoys negotiations
  — self-confidence.

3 Motivation — the negotiator operates independently and therefore needs the self-confidence and the self-starting qualities to work away from people in authority. He needs, too, motivation of a character which — as we analysed in chapter 18 — emerges as medium on achievement, medium on affiliation, medium on power.
4 Age range, too, may be important and there are certain age limits within which effective negotiators are most likely to be found.
During the early stages of a career, an individual's life style is characterised by competitive attitudes, some elements of idealism, and high concern to establish one's own position. One is concerned during these stages with gaining experience and with 'promotion prospects'.
Late stages of a career are characterised by a much higher tolerance for other people's viewpoints and by increasing commitment to domestic and social goals. No longer is success at work the outstanding criterion. In between these early and later stages there is a period in which experience has conditioned one's approach and

one's career objectives; yet energy remains at a high level and there is a continuing and important search for satisfaction from work. The precise ages for this mid-career phase vary from individual to individual, but for most people, last maybe a decade within the age range of 33-50. Desirable age range for negotiators is thus likely to be within the band 33 to 50.

After choosing the negotiator, the next aspect of personal management is *training* him.

The initial training of negotiators, assuming adequate product and technical knowledge, needs to cover:

1 Company forms and procedures.
2 Legal and trading regulations governing negotiations.
3 Basic skills of negotiating.

In practice one finds that many negotiators are appointed on the assumption that they will learn by experience and will pick up skills while on-the-job members of negotiating teams. This is wasteful – it is possible to compress a lot of experience into active training processes in which potential negotiators handle case studies of negotiations, learning a little bit about theory and a great deal more from their own achievements and failures, from their own observation of colleagues at work and from feed-back both from their colleagues and from Others with whom they have negotiated.

Much experience may be compressed into off-the-job training, but of course there still remains a need to build and test experience on the job, working with effective negotiators.

Training is also of importance to the experienced negotiator and is one of the issues to be considered in the third aspect of personal management: the *motivation* of experienced negotiators.

No negotiator will be motivated unless he feels that he has adequate salary, pension, expenses, adequate office, adequate car.

In all such valuations, 'adequate' is measured by the negotiator against some standard which he builds for himself. This standard is influenced by what he believes to be the market rate; and by what he believes to be the rewards of other people whom he sees as being of similar stature.

But these extrinsic rewards will not motivate (reference 15); they are simply factors which will de-motivate unless he is satisfied.

His positive motivation depends on intrinsic rewards.

Here is a check-list of some such intrinsic rewards, with suggestions of how to generate them for the negotiator.

> The intrinsic reward of satisfaction from the negotiations themselves:
>> It is satisfying to conduct a tough negotiation and to come out of it with a positive result. Give him tough tasks.
>
> Recognition of that achievement by the boss:
>> Make it clear to him that you value the achievement.
>
> Recognition of the achievement by others:
>> Publicise it. Do not put into the company news sheet just 'We have won an important order', but rather, 'Harry Jones has won this order for us'.

His personal satisfaction requires that he knows how the company values what he is doing; and requires too that he has the responsibility and the degrees of freedom which will stretch him and give him satisfaction.

> Personal growth — give him the chance to tackle new and interesting assignments.
>
> Personal development — give him the chance to meet other negotiators and to check with them on successes and common problems. Encourage him to meet others in working seminars; or even simply for private discussion of successes and failures. Give him at least three days a year in which to freshen his personal development.

Hopefully, then, the manager will have chosen a good negotiator, will have ensured that he is duly trained and will be ensuring too that he is well motivated. This brings us to the pattern of relationships which should exist between the boss and the negotiator.

Relationships management

Of key importance to the relationships between manager and negotiator are:

- The way in which responsibility is shared between them.
- The way in which authority is shared between them.
- The manner in which they set up common objectives.

The first requirement is that manager and individual negotiator have similar views about that negotiator's job. What he is supposed to do. His responsibilities and authorities, the procedure for planning and reviewing his activities.

In one sense this is no more than a job specification.
But not all negotiators have job specifications, and even when they have them, many job specifications are meaningless bits of paper. To make them meaningful they must reflect the style of operation of the enterprise and the style in which negotiations will be conducted.

Within a bureaucratic organisation, the negotiator needs a job specification stating precisely his responsibility and the extent and limits to his authority. This job specification should be prepared by personnel specialists, expert in the drafting of job specifications, and authorised by the manager. The job specification should be properly presented — typed and carrying a due degree of formality — regularly and formally reviewed. The job specification is then the embodiment of the way in which the negotiator should operate.

Within a more democratic organisation the job specification is used in a quite different manner. It is used as a lubricant to the relationship between the negotiator and other people — especially his boss. It is seen as providing a vehicle for manager and negotiator together to discuss what his responsibilities are; together to discuss what authority he has; together to discuss the areas in which they have joint responsibility and joint authority.

Such discussion promotes mutual understanding between manager and negotiator. Once the discussion has moved to the point of mutual understanding being achieved, then the function of producing the job specification has been largely achieved.

> The understanding developed by discussion of job specification, is very much more important in such organisations than is the job specification itself.
>
> Indeed, I know organisations where the job specification is thought of as something to be developed in such discussions on the back of an envelope and to be obsolete by the time it has been developed.

Apart from using some such means — appropriate to the character of his own organisation — to lubricate mutual understanding of responsibilities and authorities, the manager needs also to be concerned about the *objectives* of the negotiation.

The defining of objectives for a particular negotiation is a delicate responsibility for the manager and the division of that responsibility between himself and the negotiator is a sensitive issue.

> On the one hand the manager needs to assert the organisation's interest in securing the best possible deal.
>
> On the other hand, the negotiating team needs to be empowered with approprate degrees of flexibility, and they may be motivated by the freedom to set for themselves challenging objectives.

The manner in which this dilemma of delegation is resolved should reflect the operating style of the organisation. A helpful bit of theory for this purpose (reference 14) is concerned particularly with differences in types of leadership. At one extreme there is the type of leader who keeps everything in his own grasp: at the other extreme, there is the leader who is very keen on delegation. Across this range, there is a sequence of six different leadership styles:

> Tell — tell our people what to do.
> Sell — tell them what to do and why.
> Test — check whether they think it is a good idea.

Consult — consult them before deciding.
Join — join with them in making the decision.
Delegate — give guidance to help them to take decisions.

We can recognise a similar range of team leaders for negotiations. Habits of working in one or another of these styles are pervasive through organisations. Both manager and negotiator will, in their normal relationships, evolve an understanding and acceptance of a particular style. The delegation of authority between them, for objective fixing, should reflect that normal pattern.

If the organisational style is 'tell' — then the manager should tell the negotiator what objectives he is to achieve.
If the organisation style is 'delegate' — then the manager should have a general discussion with the negotiator of the purpose of the negotiations and leave him the responsibility for crystallising the aims and the targets.

Organisations at the centre of the spectrum — those with a 'test' or 'consult' style — will find it helpful to allocate responsibility for objective fixing, using the distinction we have suggested between purpose, aims and targets. For example:

the definition of purpose as a joint responsibility of senior manager and team-leader;
the definition of aims as dominantly the leader's, in consultation with manager and team;
the definition of targets, by the team in consultation with team-leader.

The relationship between the manager and the negotiator is thus one which it is important to manage effectively. We have suggested that this will be helped by adopting some processes which reconcile their views on their joint responsibility, their joint authority and, in particular, of the way in which objectives are set for the negotiations.

Organisational management

Experience shows us that in many work relationships, individuals find themselves in conflict with one another. This conflict arises from differing goals, needs, experiences, way of looking at the world.

The possibilities of conflict are increased under either of two conditions:

1 Geographical separation.
   Distance leads to disenchantment. It has been found that when a well integrated work team is split in two so that half of the team operates in a different location, then within weeks the two halves are likely to be at loggerheads.
2 Stress differences.
   The drama of negotiating is remote from the routine of everyday activities back-home. There is such a difference in the form of stress between the drama and the routine that prospects of conflict are heightened.

There is thus a need for the manager to take positive steps to ensure collaboration between the negotiating groups and the back-home team. Steps to help in sustaining teamwork despite the pressures, include:

1 Ensure that the parties recognise joint responsibility and authority:
   Make use of discussions of job specifications between negotiator and supporters in similar manner to the use between negotiator and manager.
2 Give general ownership of the negotiations:
   Involve the support team in recognising the possibilities, problems, opportunities and objectives for the negotiations.
3 Ensure overlap of expectations:
   Get the support team working with the negotiator in planning the negotiations.
4 In the case of extended negotiations, ensure ample face-to-face contact:
   Jointly monitor progress and support, check on mutual interests, and revise plans when needed.

Summary

Important matters for the managers of negotiators include:

1 Choosing negotiators with a combination of technical knowledge and specified personal characteristics.
2 The character of the negotiator should show a blend of desire for achievement, affiliation and power.
3 There is a 'most likely' age-band within which most effective negotiators will be found.
4 Negotiators need initial training, both on and off-the-job; and later opportunity for personal development and for testing themselves alongside other people of experience.
5 Motivation of negotiators by their manager demands not only extrinsic rewards: it demands job satisfaction too.
6 The manager's relationship with the negotiator can be helped by ensuring that there is common understanding of joint responsibilities, joint authority and of the process of objective setting.
7 Relationships between negotiator and support team should be lubricated by joint involvement in planning and progressing the negotiation.

20 Power, strength and influence

To conclude this book, let us consider how the negotiator can and should exercise power, strength and influence.

By *power,* we mean the capacity to dominate. It is in two forms:

1 Power of position: for example, the big government or industrial organisation negotiating with the small man.
2 Personal power — a combination of a particular personality and the use of power tactics.

Power is not usually a desirable quality for a negotiator to establish. It is only in the exceptional case that he should turn a negotiation into a battle to be won by power. Normally, if his case is naturally strong he does not need power. If his case is not naturally strong, then Others will resent his attempts to assert power and will defend themselves. The power seeker has then pushed towards warfare — not a skilful way of negotiating.

The assertion of power may be all too easily done. The man who dashes into a negotiation saying that he has very little time, is asserting power in terms of his control over time and the negotiating process: however urgent his need to catch the next plane, he is asserting that his interests are more im-

221

portant than joint interests. It is maddening.

The person who is determined to make the opening statement; the person who makes an excessively long statement; the person who specifies negotiating procedure and is not prepared to compromise in order to obtain the Other Party's agreement; the person who seeks to win any argument at the Other Party's expense: these are all seen to be power hunters.

Note that they are often making errors out of ignorance rather than out of intent. The person who does these things in his negotiating processes may be quite unaware that he is doing them, quite unaware of Other Party's reactions, quite unaware of the reasons why he fails to achieve his objectives.

So the effective negotiator is one who is aware of the reactions which he can bring about in other people, and skilled in avoiding the pitfalls in power plays.

The *strength* of a negotiator depends on the situation he is in. It depends on the combination of technical, economic and social ingredients which he represents when he comes to the negotiating table − if he is selling products which really are cheapest and best, he's in a strong position. His strength depends also on the resources backing him − the boss, the secretary, the colleagues, and the impressions created by his organisation's reputation, publicity and marketing.

The negotiator's strength depends not only on those forces, over which he has relatively little control. It depends too on the way the Other Party assesses the situation: and the assessment is one which he can influence.

His skills are in the way he develops and uses his *influence*. A basic skill in that influence is the ability to communicate: to create conditions for effective communication, present information, present cases, keep it simple, listen diligently, use the skills of non-verbal communication.

A negotiator can influence the whole pattern of a negotiation, so that it will move creatively 'Towards Agreement' in the common interests of the two parties. The great skills of that form of negotiating lie in:

1 Establishing a secure and cordial climate.
2 Getting agreement from the outset on the procedures −

the Purpose, Plan and Pace for the meeting.
3 Exploration of joint interests, clarification and creativity.
4 Keeping control of the conduct of the negotiation, helping it to move on a broad front, checking progress against agreed plans, emphasising agreement.
5 Having prepared to good effect before entering the negotiating room.

It takes great skill to establish and develop such an influence 'Towards Agreement'. It also takes great skill to influence a negotiation 'To Our Advantage'. Now we need skills in:

1 Creating a pleasant climate, and getting agreement to a plan of negotiation.
2 Preparing more firmly. Aims and targets more clearly specified.
3 Developing the ability to give the other man satisfaction whilst gaining the advantage we seek.
4 Choosing and presenting the highest defensible bid.
5 Bargaining to advantage.

Whichever pattern of negotiation is appropriate, the negotiator will need skill in two other respects:

1 The skills needed in teamwork.
2 The special skills needed in handling extensive negotiations.

In striving to exert his influence, the negotiator should not try to conform to one ideal pattern. We are all different; some of us are good at some things, some at others. Each of us naturally develops his own personal style — his own blend of skills.

And which style should he develop? I believe in making the best use of our strengths. I believe that we should each develop a style which will give prominence to our strengths, and which will not make heavy demands on skills we don't possess. That style not only gives us the scope to do what we are good at. It also avoids the positive damage which is done by adopting behaviour which is incongruent. If the quiet man starts to talk a lot, loudly, this will be recognised both by his colleagues and by Others as an act which he is putting on. If, on the other hand, the quiet man builds his skill in quietly making points and in recognising more clearly the sort of points which he is skilled in making – then his influence will increase still further.

The style which a negotiator develops will be a personal style: partly, it will be purely individual, partly it will reflect the style of the organisation he represents and the culture of the country he comes from. It should give best play for his strengths; and he will always have scope to polish some of the skills within his personal style. So – with the help of an effective boss, effective training and a suitable strategy for each negotiation – he will build his influence.

Psychology can justify and enrich our understanding of the skills. Bosses and colleagues can help us to prepare and support us when we are out in the field. But at the end of the negotiation, satisfaction does not come from forcing something onto an unwilling opponent, nor dissatisfaction from yielding to overwhelming pressure. Our sense of fulfilment comes from the conviction that we have worked with another party to create a deal excellent for us both, or from the conviction that we have earned the advantage whilst yet giving satisfaction.

Our sense of fulfilment comes from having successfully used the practical skills of negotiating.

References and further reading

1. Argyle, Michael, *The Psychology of Interpersonal Behaviour*, Pelican, 1967

   A fine summary of the way people behave and are seen to behave by one another.

2. Blake and Mouton, *The Managerial Grid*, Gulf, 1964

   This book presents one of the classic theories about different styles of managing.

3. de Bono, Edward, *The Use of Lateral Thinking*, Pelican, 1971

4. Karrass, C.L., *The Negotiating Game*, World Publishing Co., 1968

   The practical guide to the subject of negotiating from an American standpoint.

5. Karrass, C.L., *Give and Take*, World Publishing Co., 1974

   This book is all about negotiating tactics.

6. Lamb, Warren, *Posture and Gesture*, Duckworth, 1965

The classic introduction to non-verbal communication.

7. McClelland, D.C. et al., *The Achievement Motive*, Appleton-Century-Crofts, 1953

8. Marsh, P.D.V., *Contract Negotiation Handbook*, Gower, 1974

   Excellent treatment of negotiating strategy of general interest. Preceded by a mathematical/economic analysis of bidding – also excellent, but demanding a reader with mathematical talents.

9. Maslow, A.H., *Motivation and Personality*, Harper, 1954

10. Nierenberg, G.I. and Colero, H.H., *How to Read a Person like a Book*, Hawthorne, 1971

11. Nederlands Pedagogisch Instituut, *Phases in the Development of Organisations*, in 'Some Basic Concepts used in Management Seminars', 1969, NPI International Zeist, Holland

12. Salanick and Pfeffer, 'A Social Information Processing approach to attitudes, behaviour and job characteristics', in *Administration Science Quarterly*, June, 1978

13. Schein, Edgar H., *Process Consultation*, Addison-Wesley, 1969

14. Tannenbaum, A.S. et al., *Leadership and Motivation*, McGraw-Hill, 1961

15. Herzberg. F. et al., *The Motivation to Work*, Wiley, 1959

Index

227

228 THE SKILLS OF NEGOTIATIN